BEOWULF

AN ANGLO-SAXON EPIC POEM

Translated by J. LESSLIE HALL

Introduction by KEMP MALONE

Beowulf
Translated from the Heyne-Socin text by John Lesslie Hall
Introduction by Kemp Malone

Print ISBN 13: 978-1-4209-5590-3
eBook ISBN 13: 978-1-4209-5591-0

This edition copyright © 2017. Digireads.com Publishing.

Cover Image: a detail of an illustration by J. R. Skelton from "Stories of Beowulf" by H. E. Marshall, New York, E. P. Dutton & co., 1908.

Please visit *www.digireads.com*

CONTENTS

Introduction

The literary history of England falls into two great divisions, commonly called medieval and modern but better named in terms of the Protestant Reformation, an upheaval which had revolutionary effects not only on English religious life but also on English literature, as indeed on every aspect of English civilization. The works of literary art which have come down to us from the England of pre-Reformation times vary markedly, of course, in many ways, but they go together at bottom: they are rooted and grounded in the Latin Christianity which dominated the culture of western Europe from the post-classical period to the sixteenth century. The Church, however, had grown up and taken form in the midst of a powerful pagan culture, the civilization of classical antiquity, and the Roman and Irish missions of the sixth and seventh centuries planted the Church of England in the midst of another pagan culture, that of the ancient Germanic peoples. The new religion did not scorn the literary tradition either of classical or of Germanic paganism. Aldhelm, the first Englishman to compose religious verse in Latin, and Cædmon, the first Englishman to compose religious verse in English, were contemporaries, and both followed essentially the same procedure. Each sang the praises of the Christian God in an artistic medium inherited from paganism. Each poured new wine into old bottles.

In one respect, nevertheless, the two pioneers differed greatly. Christian literature in the Latin tongue was no novelty when Aldhelm and Cædmon began to sing. On the contrary, by the seventh century a large body of Latin Christian prose and verse had come into being, and Aldhelm had many Christian as well as pagan literary models at his disposal; that is to say, his task was one of imitation rather than of innovation. Cædmon, on the other hand, showed great originality, an originality which deserves the name of genius, when he seized upon the inherited native English way of composing poetry and used it in making poems Christian in theme and spirit. Nothing of the kind had ever been thought of before, so far as we know, Cædmon himself, indeed, had had no thought of such a thing in his waking hours; his inspiration came to him in sleep, and took the form of a dream, in which a messenger of God made a poet of him and told him what to sing. It took a miracle to show Caedmon and his fellows that the native English poetical technique was worthy of use in serving God. One is reminded of St. Peter's vision at Joppa, when he

saw heaven opened, and a certain vessel descending unto him, as it had been a great sheet knit at the four corners, and let down to the earth: wherein were all manner of four-footed beasts of the earth, and wild beasts, and creeping things, and fowls of the air. And there came a voice to him, Rise, Peter, kill, and eat. But Peter said, Not so, Lord; for I have never eaten any thing that is common or unclean. And the voice spake unto him again the second time, What God hath cleansed, that call not thou common. [Acts 10:11-15].

In the seventh century and for many centuries thereafter, Latin was the language of the Church of England. The Latin tongue was the tongue of God, the natural and proper medium for high and holy thoughts. English was associated with worldly matters, and the English way of making poetry in particular could hardly have been turned to religious purposes without a specific revelation from on high.

This revelation came to Cædmon, and its authenticity was duly accepted by the Church. In consequence, English poetry, from the earliest times of which we have record down to the Protestant Reformation, was predominantly religious poetry, and throughout Old English times this predominance was overwhelming. Or perhaps it would be safer to say that only a small part of the Old English verse which survives to us can be reckoned purely secular. The custom of using the vernacular, alongside Latin, for religious poetical purposes, spread to the Continent in the eighth century, thanks to the English missionaries who in that century converted the Germans to Christianity and reformed the Gallican Church. Cædmon, then, may be looked upon as the father, not only of English religious poetry, but also of the religious poetry in the vernaculars of continental Europe.

Here we are primarily concerned not with Old English religious poetry in general but with a particular poem: *Beowulf*. This poem holds a unique place in the literature of Europe. Its fundamentally Christian orientation is now widely recognized, and needs no discussion in this paper. Nevertheless, one cannot properly classify it as a religious poem in any strict or narrow sense. The action of the poem takes place in a part of ancient Germania and at a time thought of by the poet as ancient and therefore pagan. The characters are not Christians and know nothing of Christianity. The hero is a virtuous pagan. He is made as Christ-like as the setting permits, but all his virtues can be explained quite naturally as growing out of the heroic ideals of conduct traditional among the English as among the other Germanic peoples.

The monkish author, devout Christian though he is, finds much to admire in the pagan cultural tradition which, as an Englishman, he inherited from ancient Germania. It is his purpose to glorify this heroic heritage, this spiritual heirloom, this precious birthright of his nation. He accomplishes his purpose by laying stress upon those things in Germanic tradition which agree with Christianity or at any rate do not clash seriously with the Christian faith. In particular, his hero in all he says and does shows himself high-minded, gentle, and virtuous, a man dedicated to the heroic life, and the poet presents this life in terms of service: Beowulf serves his lord, his people, and all mankind, and in so doing he does not shrink from hardship, danger, and death itself. In many passages the poet's own Christianity comes to the surface, most notably, perhaps, in the so-called sermon of the aged King Hrothgar, who out of the fullness of his wisdom warns the youthful hero against the sin of pride. But even here the king's words, though obviously based on Christian teaching, are not put in specifically Christian terms, and most of the time the author keeps his Christianity below the surface. Nor does he falsify Germanic paganism by leaving out those features of it inconsistent with the Christian faith. Thus he puts in the mouth of Beowulf himself the following piece of pagan wisdom:

it is better for every man
to avenge his friend than to mourn much [1384b-1385]

The poet's picture of the Germanic past is idealized but not distorted. The devil-worship of the Danes (as the medieval Christians conceived it to be) is mentioned with perfect frankness in a famous passage (lines 175 ff.). Anachronisms are fewer and less serious than one would expect in a poem of the eighth century. Indeed, perhaps the most remarkable though not the most important feature of the poem is the relatively high standard of historical accuracy which it maintains. The author was clearly a man learned in the traditional lore of his people, and concerned to tell the truth as he saw it.

We have seen that the earliest Christian poets of England, whether they composed in Latin or in English, took over the poetical manner traditional for the language of composition (and pagan in origin) but supplied their own matter: namely, Christian story or Christian teaching. For the matter handed down in the old pagan poetry they had no use; indeed, they objected strongly to what the old poets had to say, much though they admired and imitated their way of saying it. For illustration, I shall have to limit myself to two utterances of Alcuin, an Englishman of the eighth century best known for the help he gave Charlemagne in the so-called Carolingian revival of learning. In one of his poems, Alcuin compares the Song of Songs most favorably with the poetry of Virgil, saying,

I urge you, young man, to learn these canticles by heart. They are better by far than the songs of mendacious Virgil. They sing to you the precepts of life eternal; he in his wickedness will fill your ears with worthless lies.

Alcuin condemns with equal severity the stock of traditional story drawn upon by the English scops of his day. In a letter of his he has this to say about one of these stories:

What has Ingeld to do with Christ? Narrow is the room, and it cannot hold both. The heavenly king will have nothing to do with so-called kings, heathen and damned, because that king reigns in heaven, world without end, but the heathen one, damned, laments in hell.

This attitude toward pagan literature prevailed, on the whole, down to the rise of humanism in fourteenth-century Italy. The humanists, however, found admirable in, say, Cicero, not only his artistic skill as a writer of Latin prose, but also his philosophy of life. This widening of interest served to accentuate, in the humanists, the reverence for classical antiquity so characteristic of the Middle Ages in general. The new movement brought the cult of classicism to the verge of idolatry, and humanistic thinking may be looked upon as the last and most extreme phase of medieval idealization of classical culture.

Let us now go back to the *Beowulf* poet. It would hardly do to think of him as an eighth-century humanist, six hundred years before his time, since his interest lay, not in the philosophy of life of classical antiquity but in that of Germanic antiquity. Nevertheless his case is not unlike Petrarch's in that both authors, Christians though they were, sought and found spiritual as well as stylistic values in a pagan literary culture; each in the particular culture which was his own by inheritance. In this matter the *Beowulf* poet did not stand alone. The author of *Deor* taught the virtue of patience under affliction by exempla drawn from pagan Germanic story, and the author of *Maldon* sang of a Christian lord and dright who fought and died for the faith, inspired and sustained by the same heroic ideals that their heathen forefathers had cherished. These ideals held their own to the very end of Old English times, and made many a man a hero in life and death not merely by force of ordinary tradition but also, and in large measure, by force of poetic tradition. The scops kept the old ideals strong by singing the heroes of the past. The very attack which Alcuin made on heroic story tells us that in his day the old songs were still sung even in the citadels of English Christian piety: the monasteries. Such performances became impossible, of course, after the monastic reform in the latter part of the tenth century, a reform which swept western Europe and established a more rigorous pattern of monkish life wherever it went. But the English monk of that same century who composed the poem on the Battle of Maldon still knew and loved the traditional poetry of his people, and we may be sure that he was one of many.[1]

The complex and sophisticated art of the *Beowulf* poet calls for a correspondingly elaborate analysis, an analysis which we cannot make at this time. We shall have to content ourselves here with a mere glance at the main fable or plot, before going on to a somewhat narrower study of the episodes. The action of the poem falls into two main parts. In part one, the hero Beowulf, then young, goes from his homeland to Heorot, the hall of the Danish king Hrothgar, in order to cleanse it of Grendel, a troll who for years had haunted it at night; he overcomes Grendel single-handed and afterward slays Grendel's mother, who sought to avenge her son. In part two, the hero, now grown old, goes out to defend his own kingdom against the ravages of a dragon; with the help of a faithful young kinsman he kills the dragon but himself falls in the fight. About two thirds of the poem are devoted to part one; about one third is devoted to part two. The course of events in part one takes six days; in part two, one day (excluding preliminaries in both cases), Between the two parts there is an interval of many years.

It will be seen that the poet deals in detail with two chapters only of the hero's life, and that these two chapters stand in sharp contrast. In the first, the hero is young; he is represented as an ideal retainer; he undertakes a task which he is not in duty bound to perform; full of the generous spirit of youth, he goes out of his way to do good; he fights single-handed against two foes (taken one at a time); he wins, and goes home in triumph. In the contrasting chapter, the hero is old; he is represented as an ideal king; the task he undertakes is one which he cannot avoid without failing in his duty to his own people; sad at heart, he meets the issue without flinching; he fights, with a helper beside him, against a single foe; he wins, but at the cost of his own life.

The two chapters, however, have one feature in common; in both, Beowulf fights as the champion of mankind, against monstrous embodiments of the forces of evil, adversaries so formidable that only the greatest of heroes could possibly cope with them. Our Christian poet makes much of the hero as monster-queller, not only because a fight with a monster in the nature of the case is more dangerous and therefore more heroic than a fight with another man, but also, and chiefly, because the struggle between hero and monster symbolizes the struggle between good and evil in our earthly life. Mere man-to-man fighting lends itself far less readily to treatment in terms of right and wrong, and the poet accordingly makes little of his hero's military career. Here our author goes his own way, the way of a Christian moralist, departing deliberately and radically from the practice usual in heroic story, where the hero's exploits in battle get plenty of attention.

---

[1] For further discussion, see "The Old English School," Chapter V, in Baugh, Brooke, Chew, Malone, and Sherburn, *A Literary History of England* (New York, 1948).

The poet's neglect of Beowulf's deeds of valor in ordinary warfare must have been deliberate. Certainly he was well informed about them. He tells us himself, though with the utmost brevity, about one of the many battles which his hero had survived with honor. In this particular battle, fought in the Low Countries, Beowulf had covered himself with glory: he had killed no less than thirty of the enemy in hand-to-hand conflict; one of them, the Frankish champion Dæghrefn, he slew with his bare hands. The poet informs us further that Beowulf was the only man on his side to survive the battle. His own triumph over the enemy was so complete that, though his fellows all lay dead, he held the field alone and stripped from the bodies of the thirty men he had slain the armor to which his victory over them gave him honorable title, the surviving Franks not daring to interfere and allowing him to fall back to the sea unmolested. The story of King Hygelac's ill-fated expedition to the Netherlands, and in particular the story of the last stand of the doomed army, the fall of Hygelac, and the death of man after man of the king's devoted dright, until at the end Beowulf stood alone—this was surely a fight worthy of celebration in song. The *Beowulf* poet, in four scattered passages, has something to say about the expedition and its outcome. But he fails to make even an episode of it, much less a major part of the poem. Some poets would have thought it enough for a whole epic.

But I do not wish to blame the poet for what he left undone. He knew what he was about. Hygelac's expedition had no high moral purpose. The king and his men were out for booty, and our pious poet, though he loved a good fight as well as anybody, chose for extended treatment tasks undertaken and carried through by the hero for the benefit of mankind.

One exploit of Beowulf's remains to be considered: his swimming match with Breca. This match makes a clean-cut episode, to which more than one hundred lines are devoted. The story of the match is not told as such, however. It is set in a frame: the fliting between Unferth and Beowulf. The integration of frame and story is beautifully complete: the swimming match is the subject of the fliting, each contender in the war of words giving us his own version of the story of the match. In consequence, this story is told twice. The repetition is characteristic of the *Beowulf* poet, who loves to tell a story more than once. We have already seen that Hygelac's expedition up the Rhine is spoken of no less than four times. The most elaborate piece of repetition in the poem, of course, is Beowulf's report to Hygelac when he comes back from Denmark; this report amounts to a retelling of the story of the fight with Grendel and Grendel's mother. Many other cases of repetition occur in the course of the narrative. The poet repeats himself in a masterly fashion; the device as he employs it not only emphasizes and clarifies but also gives esthetic pleasure. When we come to a given repetition we know what to expect in a general way, but we always find novelty enough in word and thought. The two versions of the swimming match differ markedly, of course, in point of view, and therefore are highly differentiated, much more so than is the case with the other repetitions in the poem.

But why does the poet make so much of the swimming match? It comes under the head of the hero's *enfances*, or exploits of boyhood, a familiar feature of heroic story, but one fundamentally trivial in character. Beowulf mentions some other boyish feats of his when he first addresses King Hrothgar. His speech begins,

Be thou hale, Hrothgar! I am Hvgelac's kinsman and retainer. I did many glorious deeds when I was a boy [lines 407-409a].

This is pretty vague, of course, but later on in the speech he tells Hrothgar, more specifically, that he had been a giant-killer, that he had taken five giants captive, that he had slain sea-monsters by night, and that he had fought with success against certain unnamed foes of his own people. Obviously if Beowulf fought monsters as well as that in his boyhood he ought to be able to cope with Grendel now that he has become a full-grown man. In other words, Beowulf's catalogue of his early exploits is meant to convince the king that here at last is the man he needs. The catalogue serves also to instruct the reader or hearers of the poem; they learn out of Beowulf's own mouth—that is, from the most authoritative source possible—that he is a redoubtable champion; in particular, that he is a monster-queller. This device of self-characterization is familiar in literary art. One finds it in Shakespeare, for example. The *Beowulf* poet's use of it is, in all likelihood, highly traditional and conventional.

Beowulf's mention of sea-monsters which he had slain by night takes us back to the swimming match with Breca, one detail of which is precisely this monster-quelling on the part of the hero. The quelling, as Beowulf himself points out, is of benefit to mankind, and may be taken for a kind of prelude to the more important quelling which is to follow at the Danish court. But after all, the two boys, when they agreed and vowed to swim to sea, had no thought of rendering a service to their fellow men. They risked their lives in this swimming match on the high seas in a spirit of recklessness. They were showing off. In Beowulf's story of the swim we catch the apologetic note: "we were both still in our boyhood" [530b-537a], he says. The implication is clear that the Beowulf who had reached young manhood would not have undertaken such a match. One should not risk one's life in vain.

It now becomes clearer why the poet makes a good deal of the swimming match. The story of the match gives us a short but vivid view of the adolescent hero in action. We get other glimpses of him as a boy, but nowhere else is any event of his boyhood told in detail. The poet reserves the main fable for his hero as a young man and as an old man, but in one episode he presents him in his immaturity. Here the future champion of mankind against the world of monsters is already a monster-queller, though not yet informed with a high moral purpose. He plays with the heroic life to which, later on, he will dedicate himself in earnest.

Most of the episodic matter in the poem, however, is concerned not with the hero himself but with his setting. The author, as we have seen, was not only a Christian moralist. He was also an Englishman; that is, a man of Germanic stock and traditions. He chose a hero of his own race, and gave him for setting the golden age of ancient Germania, that glorious period of migration when the Germanic tribes overran the Roman Empire and made its provinces into Germanic kingdoms. A well-known American scholar, after remarking upon the intense patriotism characteristic of the English, adds,

It is very surprising, then, in turning to the oldest English epic, to find that there is nothing patriotic about it at all. We call it an English poem, and rightly. It was written on English soil, for Englishmen, and in the English tongue. . . . Yet the epic deals neither with English people nor with English heroes. . . . The peoples whom it celebrates are foreigners, Scandinavians. . . . In short, *Beowulf* is a story dealing with foreign subject-matter, borrowed from an alien and even hostile people, with no trace of English patriotism about it. How is this strange situation to be explained?[2]

Our answer must be that the question is ill conceived, arising as it does out of a mistaken view of eighth-century England. In those days the English, so far as their culture was concerned, still belonged, in part, to a commonwealth of nations, the Germania of their Continental forefathers. Within that commonwealth they were at home, and felt the Goth, the Swede, the Langobard alike to be cultural fellow-countrymen. The *Beowulf* poet was intensely patriotic; his poem shows at every turn the warmth of his love for his native culture and his native race. But his patriotism embraced Germania as a whole; it was no narrowly English affair. It is particularly significant, I think, that his hero lived and died in southern Scandinavia, the heart of the old Germanic homeland, the cradle of the race, the region least affected by foreign influences. Moreover, it was from the Jutland peninsula, a part of this very region, that the English themselves had come, in their great migration to Britain. We must not forget that England in its earliest centuries was still colonial territory. The stream of settlers from the

---

[2] W. W. Lawrence, Medieval Story, p. 30.

Germanic motherland had probably stopped flowing by the time of the *Beowulf* poet, but the English had not forgotten their origin nor yet the source of their cultural traditions. Above all, *Beowulf* is a poem of the past, of a past thought of by the poet as remote. The action of such a poem obviously must take place in the homeland, not in a colony of recent foundation.

It may be worth our while, however, to speculate about the poet's reasons for not making King Offa the hero of his poem. Offa is the only English king of the Continental period about whom we have much information. We learn of him both in *Beowulf* and in *Widsith*. The *Beowulf* poet calls him the best of all mankind, and adds that he was held in high esteem far and wide because of his generosity and his success in warfare. The poet also tells us that Offa ruled his country with wisdom. In *Widsith* we get more specific information about Offa's achievements: while still a boy he overthrew "with single sword" (that is, by his own efforts, without help from others) the kingdom of the Myrgings, and dictated a boundary between his own kingdom and theirs, a boundary which his successors were able to keep. Moreover, we have reason to think that Offa was the first English king whose realm included western as well as eastern Sleswiek. As I have said elsewhere,

The extension of the English king's authority to the North Sea coast of Sleswiek made possible the later migration of the Angles to Britain, a migration which obviously would never have taken place had the English holdings remained strictly Baltic. Offa's war with the Myrgings, then, must be reckoned one of the great turning-points of English history. . . .

It seems clear that Offa was a man eminently suitable for celebration in song. An English poet in particular might be expected to make Offa the hero of a poem set in the Germania of the migration period, the heroic age of the Germanic peoples. Why did our poet choose Beowulf instead? The answer, I think, is simple. Beowulf was famous chiefly as a queller of monsters, whereas Offa won his fame as a queller of men. The poet, pious Christian that he was, found spiritual values in Beowulf's monster-quelling which he could not find in Offa's man-quelling. Nevertheless he did not like to leave Offa out of his poem altogether. The great hero of his own tribe must be brought in somehow. The episode in which Offa figures I describe elsewhere as having been introduced by a *tour de force*, and this may well be a correct statement of the case. But the poet's technique of linkage here has a parallel in at least one other episode, I will take up Offa first.

King Offa is introduced not directly but by way of his wife, Queen Thrytho, and most of the episode is devoted to the lady, whose unorthodox behavior makes her more interesting than her pattern of a husband. The introduction of a husband through his wife, however, is certainly no *tour de force*. It is the introduction of Thrytho herself which makes trouble for modern readers. The poet gets her in by contrasting her with Hygd, wife of King Hygelac. Beowulf has come back home after his Grendel adventure and is approaching Hygelac's hall to make his report of the journey. The author stops at this point to comment on the hall, the king, and the king's wife. But he disposes of hall and king in a line and a half; Queen Hygd is the one he gives most of his attention to. She is characterized in accordance with the etymology of her name. *Hygd* means 'thought' and the queen is represented as thoughtful indeed: wise, well behaved, and mindful of other people's wishes and feelings. The poet explains Hygd's exemplary conduct as the fruit of deliberation, study, mental activity. He says,

The good queen of the people [i.e., Hygd] bore in mind (wæg) the haughtiness, the terrible violence of Thrytho [lines 1931b-1932].

In other words, Hygd took warning by the example of Thrytho. She took care to behave differently. This brings the poet to Thrytho's own behavior, which was certainly not very encouraging to would-be suitors, for she objected so strongly to the attentions of men that if one of them so much as looked at her she had him put to death. The poet goes on to say, "that is no way for a lady to do." We learn, however, that Thrytho turned over a new leaf after her marriage to Offa, whom she loved dearly. King Offa, it would seem, proved master of the situation at home as well as on the field of battle.

　　Linkage by contrast also serves to bring in the second Heremod passage (lines 1709-1722), a part of the so-called sermon of Hrothgar. The aged king after praising Beowulf speaks of Heremod as Beowulf's antithesis. He brings the passage to an end by exhorting Beowulf to profit by the evil example that Heremod has set. The sad fate of Heremod should be a lesson to the young hero. The same device of contrast is used in the first Heremod passage (lines 901-915), but here this type of linkage comes at the end of the passage; the poet, by contrasting Heremod with Beowulf, brings the narrative back to his hero. This passage about Heremod is introduced by the use of a different device; sequence in time. The poet has been speaking of the famous hero Sigemund, the dragon-slayer. He shifts to Heremod very simply, saying that Sigemund flourished after Heremod had had his day. We get no hint that the two men are connected in any other way, and the device which serves to link them in the poem strikes us as artificial enough. In this ease, however, the Scandinavian evidence makes it clear that Sigemund and Heremod were traditionally associated, though just what the association was we are unable to make out. This information, gained from a study of Icelandic poetry, forces us to revise our opinion of the artistic technique of the *Beowulf* poet. We now see that the true linkage between Sigemund and Heremod was left unexpressed and needed no expression, since it was already firmly fixed by tradition in the minds of the poet's audience, to be evoked at will by a mere mention of the names. It is our misfortune, but not the poet's fault, that we in our ignorance miss the true link and have to depend altogether on that sequence in time which the poet uses, as an external device only, in proceeding from the one member of the heroic pair to the other.

The device of contrast, too, now begins to have a different look. One may well suspect, though one certainly cannot prove, that the coupling of Beowulf and Heremod, and of Hygd and Thrytho, belong to tradition and have their roots deep in Germanic story. If so, the English poet took up these characters together, not as a mere device for changing the subject, but because they went together in the songs that had come down to him, the sources he drew upon for the tale he had to tell.

What functions do the episodes have in the economy of the poem? I have already said that most of them bring out the setting in which the hero lived and died. This setting was ancient Germania; more particularly, the Scandinavia of the fifth and sixth centuries of our era. The story of Scyld, mythical founder of the Danish royal house, gives us a taste of an old legend, and the description of his funeral takes us back to pagan rites dim with antiquity. The tale of Ecgtheow's feud with the avengers of Heatholaf makes the father of the hero more than a name to us and links him with the Wulfing tribe, famous in heroic story from Iceland to the Mediterranean. When Hrothgar's scop, after singing Beowulf's praises, goes on to the exploits of Sigemund, he puts our hero side by side with a hero of Frankish legend, one of the chief figures of Germanic story. That night the scop sang once more; this time he told the tale of Finn, an ancient story very welcome at the Danish court, since it ends with a Danish victory. The tale of Ingeld the English poet puts in the mouth of Beowulf himself, as part of his report to Hygelac on the state of Denmark. All these passages serve to make our hero part and parcel of the heroic age of Germanic antiquity.

It is possible, however, to make a distinction here between those episodes which have been drawn into the narrative and those that remain external to it. Examples of the former are the passages about Scyld, Ecgtheow, and the swimming match; examples of the latter are the passages about Sigemund, Finn, and Ingeld. In part two of the poem the integration of the historical passages into the story of the dragon fight has been done in such a way as to disturb many modern readers. Thus, Klaeber says (*Beowulf*, 3d ed., p. liv),

The facts of Geatish history, it cannot be denied, are a little too much in evidence and retard the narrative . . . rather seriously.

This verdict does less than justice to the narrative art of the poet, who in part two tells the story of his hero's tribe: past, present and future. The attack of the dragon on that tribe, and Beowulf's counter-attack, ending in the death both of the hero and of his monstrous antagonist, make part of the tribal story, a part which we may call the present crisis (present, that is, from the point of view of the hero). The poet gives us his account of this crisis not continuously but in sections, sections which alternate with accounts of earlier crises in the tribe's history. The death of the dragon ends the present crisis, but the messenger of Wiglaf foresees disaster for the tribe in the future, now that they have lost their great king. He justifies his forebodings by reminding his hearers of certain events of the past, events which in due course will lead to ruin, want, and exile. The poet himself adds that the messenger's fears are fully justified. The poem ends in the present, with the funeral of the hero.

It will be seen that the author of *Beowulf* in part two of his poem uses a technique of alternation between events of the present and events of the past. He restricts himself throughout to his hero's own tribe, in marked contrast to his procedure in part one, where he ranges widely over Germania. The unity of part two, in theme and form alike, is noteworthy. As for the technique of alternation which the poet uses to drive home this unity, it is a technique very familiar today, especially in the narrative art of screen and novel. Many recent screen plays follow this method of shifting repeatedly from present to past. In Hollywood they have a name for the shift backwards in time: they call it a flashback. A recent novel, *Raintree County*, by Ross Lockridge, makes systematic use of the flashback technique. In the novel, just as in part two of *Beowulf*, the action is restricted to one day, but the flashbacks take us deep into the past. It is not likely that the novelists and scenario writers of today learned this technique by studying *Beowulf*, but theirs is the technique of the *Beowulf* poet none the less.

The shift from present to past occurs three times in the narrative of part two. The poet makes the transition in a different way each time. In all three cases he manages the shift with great skill. The second transition is of special interest, as an example of the poet's craftsmanship. Beowulf and his little band of men had reached the immediate neighborhood of the dragon's lair. Beowulf was to go forward alone from that point. He sat down on the headland, and bade his followers goodbye. The aged king fell to thinking about his childhood and youth, and began to talk. His reminiscences take up nearly one hundred lines of verse. The technique seems almost realistic here. What could be more natural than for an old man to talk about old times?

One may now ask whether the three long passages on the history of the Geatas incorporated in part two should really be looked upon as episodic. Without them the story of the dragon fight would remain, but would lose greatly in spiritual quality, since we should not know as we do the people for whom Beowulf was giving his life. As the poem stands, the fate of the hero and the fate of the tribe are bound together in such a way that each lends weight and worth to the other. We mourn for the Geatas as well as for their king, and this double mourning deepens as well as widens the sweep of the tragic march of events. One cannot doubt that the poet meant it so. For him, Beowulf would not have been a hero if he had not had a people to die for. The *Beowulf* poet was above all a patriotic poet.

We end as we began, with a look at the poem taken in the large. As we have seen, *Beowulf* falls into two parts, devoted respectively to the hero in young manhood and the hero in old age. Part one is predominantly cheerful in tone, as befits a period of youth. When one reads the Sigemund episode, for instance, one feels that it is good to be alive in a world made for heroic adventure. Even the Finn episode has a happy ending if one sides with the Danes, as our poet does. Now and then the shadows of feuds that are to come darken the picture of the Danish court, and the aged Hrothgar is fond of talking about his own troubles and those of others, but the hero takes all this in his stride and goes home in triumph, leaving a cleansed and happy Heorot behind him.

Utterly different is the tone of part two. Old age has come, and death is near at hand from the start. No longer does the hero leave home, to fight the good fight in other lands. He stands strictly on the defensive. He is sad at heart; his breast surges with dark thoughts. But there is one thought which he does not have. It does not occur to him to give up. Great though the odds against him, he takes the field and fights to the last. In this world defeat and death are sure to come in the end. The hero is he who, like Beowulf, faces the worst without flinching and dies that others may live.

KEMP MALONE

1953.

Preface

The present work is a modest effort to reproduce approximately, in modern measures, the venerable epic, Beowulf. *Approximately*, I repeat; for a very close reproduction of Anglo-Saxon verse would, to a large extent, be prose to a modern ear.

The Heyne-Socin text and glossary have been closely followed. Occasionally a deviation has been made, but always for what seemed good and sufficient reason. The translator does not aim to be an editor. Once in a while, however, he has added a conjecture of his own to the emendations quoted from the criticisms of other students of the poem.

This work is addressed to two classes of readers. From both of these alike the translator begs sympathy and co-operation. The Anglo-Saxon scholar he hopes to please by adhering faithfully to the original. The student of English literature he aims to interest by giving him, in modern garb, the most ancient epic of our race. This is a bold and venturesome undertaking; and yet there must be some students of the Teutonic past willing to follow even a daring guide, if they may read in modern phrases of the sorrows of Hrothgar, of the prowess of Beowulf, and of the feelings that stirred the hearts of our forefathers in their primeval homes.

In order to please the larger class of readers, a regular cadence has been used, a measure which, while retaining the essential characteristics of the original, permits the reader to see ahead of him in reading.

Perhaps every Anglo-Saxon scholar has his own theory as to how Beowulf should be translated. Some have given us prose versions of what we believe to be a great poem. Is it any reflection on our honored Kemble and Arnold to say that their translations fail to show a layman that Beowulf is justly called our first *epic*? Of those translators who have used verse, several have written from what would seem a mistaken point of view. Is it proper, for instance, that the grave and solemn speeches of Beowulf and Hrothgar be put in ballad measures, tripping lightly and airily along? Or, again, is it fitting that the rough martial music of Anglo-Saxon verse be interpreted to us in the smooth measures of modern blank verse? Do we hear what has been beautifully called "the clanging tread of a warrior in mail"?

Of all English translations of Beowulf, that of Professor Garnett alone gives any adequate idea of the chief characteristics of this great Teutonic epic.

The measure used in the present translation is believed to be as near a reproduction of the original as modern English affords. The cadences closely resemble those used by Browning in some of his most striking poems. The four stresses of the Anglo-Saxon verse are retained, and as much thesis and anacrusis is allowed as is consistent with a regular cadence. Alliteration has been used to a large extent; but it was thought that modern ears would hardly tolerate it on every line. End-rhyme has been used occasionally; internal rhyme, sporadically. Both have some warrant in Anglo-Saxon poetry. (For end-rhyme, see 1 $_{53}$, 1 $_{54}$; for internal rhyme, 2 $_{21}$, 6 $_{40}$.)

What Gummere[3] calls the "rime-giver" has been studiously kept; viz., the first accented syllable in the second half-verse always carries the alliteration; and the last accented syllable alliterates only sporadically. Alternate alliteration is occasionally used as in the original. (See 7 $_{61}$, 8 $_5$.)

No two accented syllables have been brought together, except occasionally after a cæsural pause. (See 2 $_{19}$ and 12 $_1$.) Or, scientifically speaking, Sievers's C type has been avoided as not consonant with the plan of translation. Several of his types, however, constantly occur; *e.g.* A and a variant ($\underline{/}$ x | / x) ($\underline{/}$ x x | $\underline{/}$ x); B and a variant (x $\underline{/}$ | x $\underline{/}$) (x x $\underline{/}$ | x $\underline{/}$); a variant of D ($\underline{/}$ x | $\underline{/}$ x x); E (/ x x | $\underline{/}$). Anacrusis gives further variety to the types used in the translation.

The parallelisms of the original have been faithfully preserved. (*E.g.*, 1 $_{16}$ and 1 $_{17}$: "Lord" and "Wielder of Glory"; 1 $_{30}$, 1 $_{31}$, 1 $_{32}$; 2 $_{12}$ and 2 $_{13}$; 2 $_{27}$ and 2 $_{28}$; 3 $_5$ and 3 $_6$.) Occasionally, some loss has been sustained; but, on the other hand, a gain has here and there been made.

The effort has been made to give a decided flavor of archaism to the translation. All words not in keeping with the spirit of the poem have been avoided. Again, though many archaic words have been used, there are none, it is believed, which are not found in standard modern poetry.

With these preliminary remarks, it will not be amiss to give an outline of the story of the poem.

THE STORY

Hrothgar, king of the Danes, or Scyldings, builds a great mead-hall, or palace, in which he hopes to feast his liegemen and to give them presents. The joy of king and retainers is, however, of short duration. Grendel, the monster, is seized with hateful jealousy. He cannot brook the sounds of joyance that reach him down in his fen-dwelling near the hall. Oft and anon he goes to the joyous building, bent on direful mischief. Thane after thane is ruthlessly carried off and devoured, while no one is found strong enough and bold enough to cope with the monster. For twelve years he persecutes Hrothgar and his vassals.

Over sea, a day's voyage off, Beowulf, of the Geats, nephew of

---

[3] *Handbook of Poetics*, page 175, 1st edition.

Higelac, king of the Geats, hears of Grendel's doings and of Hrothgar's misery. He resolves to crush the fell monster and relieve the aged king. With fourteen chosen companions, he sets sail for Dane-land. Reaching that country, he soon persuades Hrothgar of his ability to help him. The hours that elapse before night are spent in beer-drinking and conversation. When Hrothgar's bedtime comes he leaves the hall in charge of Beowulf, telling him that never before has he given to another the absolute wardship of his palace. All retire to rest, Beowulf, as it were, sleeping upon his arms.

Grendel comes, the great march-stepper, bearing God's anger. He seizes and kills one of the sleeping warriors. Then he advances towards Beowulf. A fierce and desperate hand-to-hand struggle ensues. No arms are used, both combatants trusting to strength and hand-grip. Beowulf tears Grendel's shoulder from its socket, and the monster retreats to his den, howling and yelling with agony and fury. The wound is fatal.

The next morning, at early dawn, warriors in numbers flock to the hall Heorot, to hear the news. Joy is boundless. Glee runs high. Hrothgar and his retainers are lavish of gratitude and of gifts.

Grendel's mother, however, comes the next night to avenge his death. She is furious and raging. While Beowulf is sleeping in a room somewhat apart from the quarters of the other warriors, she seizes one of Hrothgar's favorite counsellors, and carries him off and devours him. Beowulf is called. Determined to leave Heorot entirely purified, he arms himself, and goes down to look for the female monster. After traveling through the waters many hours, he meets her near the sea-bottom. She drags him to her den. There he sees Grendel lying dead. After a desperate and almost fatal struggle with the woman, he slays her, and swims upward in triumph, taking with him Grendel's head.

Joy is renewed at Heorot. Congratulations crowd upon the victor. Hrothgar literally pours treasures into the lap of Beowulf; and it is agreed among the vassals of the king that Beowulf will be their next liegelord.

Beowulf leaves Dane-land. Hrothgar weeps and laments at his departure.

When the hero arrives in his own land, Higelac treats him as a distinguished guest. He is the hero of the hour.

Beowulf subsequently becomes king of his own people, the Geats. After he has been ruling for fifty years, his own neighborhood is wofully harried by a fire-spewing dragon. Beowulf determines to kill him. In the ensuing struggle both Beowulf and the dragon are slain. The grief of the Geats is inexpressible. They determine, however, to leave nothing undone to honor the memory of their lord. A great funeral-pyre is built, and his body is burnt. Then a memorial-barrow is made, visible from a great distance, that sailors afar may be constantly

reminded of the prowess of the national hero of Geatland.
The poem closes with a glowing tribute to his bravery, his
gentleness, his goodness of heart, and his generosity.

It is the devout desire of this translator to hasten the day when the
story of Beowulf shall be as familiar to English-speaking peoples as
that of the Iliad. Beowulf is our first great epic. It is an epitomized
history of the life of the Teutonic races. It brings vividly before us our
forefathers of pre-Alfredian eras, in their love of war, of sea, and of
adventure.

My special thanks are due to Professors Francis A. March and
James A. Harrison, for advice, sympathy, and assistance.

J. L. HALL.

Williamsburg, Va., Nov. 1, 1891.

Abbreviations Used in the Notes

B. = Bugge. C. = Cosijn. Gr. = Grein. Grdvtg. = Grundtvig. H. =
Heyne. H. and S. = Harrison and Sharp. H.-So. = Heyne-Socin. K.=
Kemble. Kl. = Kluge. M.= Müllenhoff. R. = Rieger. S. = Sievers. Sw. =
Sweet. t. B. = ten Brink. Th. = Thorpe. W. = Wülcker.

Bibliography of Translations

Arnold, Thomas.—Beowulf. A heroic poem of the eighth century. London, 1876. With English translation. Prose.

Botkine, L.—Beowulf. Epopée Anglo-Saxonne. Havre, 1877. First French translation. Passages occasionally omitted.

Conybeare, J.J.—Illustrations of Anglo-Saxon Poetry. London, 1826. Full Latin translation, and some passages translated into English blank-verse.

Ettmüller, L.—Beowulf, stabreimend übersetzt. Zürich, 1840.

Garnett, J.M.—Beowulf: an Anglo-Saxon Poem, and the Fight at Finnsburg. Boston, 1882. An accurate line-for-line translation, using alliteration occasionally, and sometimes assuming a metrical cadence.

Grein, C.W.M.—Dichtungen der Angelsachsen, stabreimend übersetzt. 2 Bde. Göttingen, 1857-59.

Grion, Giusto.—Beovulf, poema epico anglo-sassone del VII. secolo, tradotto e illustrato. Lucca, 1883. First Italian translation.

Grundtvig, N.F.S.—Bjowulfs Drape. Copenhagen, 1820.

Heyne, M.—A translation in iambic measures. Paderborn, 1863.

Kemble, J.M.—The Anglo-Saxon Poems of Beowulf, the Traveller's Song, and the Battle of Finnsburg. London, 1833. The second edition contains a prose translation of Beowulf.

Leo, H.—Ueber Beowulf. Halle, 1839. Translations of extracts.

Lumsden, H.W.—Beowulf, translated into modern rhymes. London, 1881. Ballad measures. Passages occasionally omitted.

Sandras, G.S.—De carminibus Cædmoni adjudicatis. Paris, 1859. An extract from Beowulf, with Latin translation.

Schaldmose, F.—Beowulf og Scopes Widsith, to Angelsaxiske Digte. Copenhagen, 1847.

Simrock, K.—Beowulf. Uebersetzt und erläutert. Stuttgart und Augsburg, 1859. Alliterative measures.

Thorkelin, G.J.—De Danorum rebus gestis secul. III. et IV. poema Danicum dialecto Anglosaxonica. Havniæ, 1815. Latin translation.

Thorpe, B.—The Anglo-Saxon Poems of Beowulf, the Scôp or Gleeman's Tale, and the Fight at Finnsburg. Oxford, 1855. English translation in short lines, generally containing two stresses.

Wackerbarth, A.D.—Beowulf, translated into English verse. London, 1849.

Wickberg, R.—Beowulf, en fornengelsk hjeltedikt, öfersatt. Westervik. First Swedish translation.

von Wolzogen, H.—Beowulf, in alliterative measures. Leipzig.

Zinsser, G.—Der Kampf Beowulfs mit Grendel. Jahresbericht of the Realschule at Forbach, 1881.

Glossary of Proper Names

[The figures refer to the divisions of the poem in which the respective names occur. The large figures refer to fitts, the small, to lines in the fitts.]

Ælfhere.—A kinsman of Wiglaf.—36 3.

Æschere.—Confidential friend of King Hrothgar. Elder brother of Yrmenlaf. Killed by Grendel.—21 3; 30 89.

Beanstan.—Father of Breca.—9 26.

Beowulf.—Son of Scyld, the founder of the dynasty of Scyldings. Father of Healfdene, and grandfather of Hrothgar.—1 18; 2 1.

Beowulf.—The hero of the poem. Sprung from the stock of Geats, son of Ecgtheow. Brought up by his maternal grandfather Hrethel, and figuring in manhood as a devoted liegeman of his uncle Higelac. A hero from his youth. Has the strength of thirty men. Engages in a swimming-match with Breca. Goes to the help of Hrothgar against the monster Grendel. Vanquishes Grendel and his mother. Afterwards becomes king of the Geats. Late in life attempts to kill a fire-spewing dragon, and is slain. Is buried with great honors. His memorial mound.—6 26; 7 2; 7 9; 9 3; 9 8; 12 28; 12 43; 23 1, etc.

Breca.—Beowulf's opponent in the famous swimming-match.—9 8; 9 19; 9 21; 9 22.

Brondings.—A people ruled by Breca.—9 23.

Brosinga mene.—A famous collar once owned by the Brosings.—19 7.

Cain.—Progenitor of Grendel and other monsters.—2 56; 20 11.

Dæghrefn.—A warrior of the Hugs, killed by Beowulf.—35 40.

Danes.—Subjects of Scyld and his descendants, and hence often called Scyldings. Other names for them are Victory-Scyldings, Honor-Scyldings, Armor-Danes, Bright-Danes, East-Danes, West-Danes, North-Danes, South-Danes, Ingwins, Hrethmen.—1 1; 2 1; 3 2; 5 14; 7 1, etc.

Ecglaf.—Father of Unferth, who taunts Beowulf.—9 1.

Ecgtheow.—Father of Beowulf, the hero of the poem. A widely-known Wægmunding warrior. Marries Hrethel's daughter. After slaying Heatholaf, a Wylfing, he flees his country.—7 3; 5 6; 8 4.

Ecgwela.—A king of the Danes before Scyld.—25 60.

Elan.—Sister of Hrothgar, and probably wife of Ongentheow, king of the Swedes.—2 10.

Eagle Cape.—A promontory in Geat-land, under which took place Beowulf's last encounter.—41 87.

Eadgils.—Son of Ohthere and brother of Eanmund.—34 2.

Eanmund.—Son of Ohthere and brother of Eadgils. The reference to these brothers is vague, and variously understood. Heyne supposes as follows: Raising a revolt against their father, they are obliged to leave Sweden. They go to the land of the Geats; with what intention, is not known, but probably to conquer and plunder. The Geatish king, Heardred, is slain by one of the brothers, probably Eanmund.—36 $_{10}$; 31 $_{54}$ to 31 $_{60}$; 33 $_{66}$ to 34 $_6$.

Eofor.—A Geatish hero who slays Ongentheow in war, and is rewarded by Hygelac with the hand of his only daughter.—41 $_{18}$; 41 $_{48}$.

Eormenric.—A Gothic king, from whom Hama took away the famous Brosinga mene.—19 $_9$.

Eomær.—Son of Offa and Thrytho, king and queen of the Angles.—28 $_{69}$.

Finn.—King of the North-Frisians and the Jutes. Marries Hildeburg. At his court takes place the horrible slaughter in which the Danish general, Hnæf, fell. Later on, Finn himself is slain by Danish warriors.—17 $_{18}$; 17 $_{30}$; 17 $_{44}$; 18 $_4$; 18 $_{23}$.

Fin-land.—The country to which Beowulf was driven by the currents in his swimming-match.—10 $_{22}$.

Fitela.—Son and nephew of King Sigemund, whose praises are sung in XIV.—14 $_{42}$; 14 $_{53}$.

Folcwalda.—Father of Finn.—17 $_{38}$.

Franks.—Introduced occasionally in referring to the death of Higelac.—19 $_{19}$; 40 $_{21}$; 40 $_{24}$.

Frisians.—A part of them are ruled by Finn. Some of them were engaged in the struggle in which Higelac was slain.—17 $_{20}$; 17 $_{42}$; 17 $_{52}$; 40 $_{21}$.

Freaware.—Daughter of King Hrothgar. Married to Ingeld, a Heathobard prince.—29 $_{60}$; 30 $_{32}$.

Froda.—King of the Heathobards, and father of Ingeld.—29 $_{62}$.

Garmund.—Father of Offa.—28 $_{71}$.

Geats, Geatmen.—The race to which the hero of the poem belongs. Also called Weder-Geats, or Weders, War-Geats, Sea-Geats. They are ruled by Hrethel, Hæthcyn, Higelac, and Beowulf.—4 $_7$; 7 $_4$; 10 $_{45}$; 11 $_8$; 27 $_{14}$; 28 $_8$.

Gepids.—Named in connection with the Danes and Swedes.—35 $_{34}$.

Grendel.—A monster of the race of Cain. Dwells in the fens and moors. Is furiously envious when he hears sounds of joy in Hrothgar's palace. Causes the king untold agony for years. Is finally conquered by Beowulf, and dies of his wound. His hand and arm are hung up in Hrothgar's hall Heorot. His head is cut off by Beowulf when he goes down to fight with Grendel's mother.—2 $_{50}$; 3 $_1$; 3 $_{13}$; 8 $_{19}$; 11 $_{17}$; 12 $_2$; 13 $_{27}$; 15 $_3$.

Guthlaf.—A Dane of Hnæf's party.—18 $_{24}$.

Half-Danes.—Branch of the Danes to which Hnæf belonged.—17 $_{19}$.

Halga.—Surnamed the Good. Younger brother of Hrothgar.—2 $_9$.

Hama.—Takes the Brosinga mene from Eormenric.—19 $_7$.

Hæreth.—Father of Higelac's queen, Hygd.—28 $_{39}$; 29 $_{18}$.

Hæthcyn.—Son of Hrethel and brother of Higelac. Kills his brother Herebeald accidentally. Is slain at Ravenswood, fighting against Ongentheow.—34 $_{43}$; 35 $_{23}$; 40 $_{32}$.

Helmings.—The race to which Queen Wealhtheow belonged.—10 $_{63}$.

Heming.—A kinsman of Garmund, perhaps nephew.—28 $_{54}$; 28 $_{70}$.

Hengest.—A Danish leader. Takes command on the fall of Hnæf.—17 $_{33}$; 17 $_{41}$.

Herebeald.—Eldest son of Hrethel, the Geatish king, and brother of Higelac. Killed by his younger brother Hæthcyn.—34 $_{43}$; 34 $_{47}$.

Heremod.—A Danish king of a dynasty before the Scylding line. Was a source of great sorrow to his people.—14 $_{64}$; 25 $_{59}$.

Hereric.—Referred to as uncle of Heardred, but otherwise unknown.—31 $_{60}$.

Hetwars.—Another name for the Franks.—33 $_{51}$.

Healfdene.—Grandson of Scyld and father of Hrothgar. Ruled the Danes long and well.—2 $_5$; 4 $_1$; 8 $_{14}$.

Heardred.—Son of Higelac and Hygd, king and queen of the Geats. Succeeds his father, with Beowulf as regent. Is slain by the sons of Ohthere.—31 $_{56}$; 33 $_{63}$; 33 $_{75}$.

Heathobards.—Race of Lombards, of which Froda is king. After Froda falls in battle with the Danes, Ingeld, his son, marries Hrothgar's daughter, Freaware, in order to heal the feud.—30 $_1$; 30 $_6$.

Heatholaf.—A Wylfing warrior slain by Beowulf's father.—8 $_5$.

Heathoremes.—The people on whose shores Breca is cast by the waves during his contest with Beowulf.—9 $_{21}$.

Heorogar.—Elder brother of Hrothgar, and surnamed 'Weoroda Ræswa,' Prince of the Troopers.—2 $_9$; 8 $_{12}$.

Hereward.—Son of the above.—31 $_{17}$.

Heort, Heorot.—The great mead-hall which King Hrothgar builds. It is invaded by Grendel for twelve years. Finally cleansed by Beowulf, the Geat. It is called Heort on account of the hart-antlers which decorate it.—2 $_{25}$; 3 $_{32}$; 3 $_{52}$.

Hildeburg.—Wife of Finn, daughter of Hoce, and related to Hnæf,—probably his sister.—17 $_{21}$; 18 $_{34}$.

Hnæf.—Leader of a branch of the Danes called Half-Danes. Killed in the struggle at Finn's castle.—17 $_{19}$; 17 $_{61}$.

Hondscio.—One of Beowulf's companions. Killed by Grendel just before Beowulf grappled with that monster.—30 $_{43}$.

Hoce.—Father of Hildeburg and probably of Hnæf.—17 $_{26}$.

Hrethel.—King of the Geats, father of Higelac, and grandfather of Beowulf.—7 $_4$; 34 $_{39}$.

Hrethla.—Once used for Hrethel.—7 $_{82}$.

Hrethmen.—Another name for the Danes.—7 $_{73}$.

Hrethric.—Son of Hrothgar.—18 65; 27 19.

Hreosna-beorh.—A promontory in Geat-land, near which Ohthere's sons made plundering raids.—35 $_{18}$.

Hrothgar.—The Danish king who built the hall Heort, but was long unable to enjoy it on account of Grendel's persecutions. Marries Wealhtheow, a Helming lady. Has two sons and a daughter. Is a typical Teutonic king, lavish of gifts. A devoted liegelord, as his lamentations over slain liegemen prove. Also very appreciative of kindness, as is shown by his loving gratitude to Beowulf.—2 $_9$; 2 $_{12}$; 4 $_1$; 8 $_{10}$; 15 $_1$; etc., etc.

Hrothmund.—Son of Hrothgar.—18 $_{65}$.

Hrothulf.—Probably a son of Halga, younger brother of Hrothgar. Certainly on terms of close intimacy in Hrothgar's palace.—16 $_{26}$; 18 $_{57}$.

Hrunting.—Unferth's sword, lent to Beowulf.—22 $_{71}$; 25 $_9$.

Hugs.—A race in alliance with the Franks and Frisians at the time of Higelac's fall.—35 $_{41}$.

Hun.—A Frisian warrior, probably general of the Hetwars. Gives Hengest a beautiful sword.—18 $_{19}$.

Hunferth.—Sometimes used for Unferth.

Hygelac, Higelac.—King of the Geats, uncle and liegelord of Beowulf, the hero of the poem.—His second wife is the lovely Hygd, daughter of Hæreth. The son of their union is Heardred. Is slain in a war with the Hugs, Franks, and Frisians combined. Beowulf is regent, and afterwards king of the Geats.—4 $_6$; 5 $_4$; 28 $_{34}$; 29 $_9$; 29 $_{21}$; 31 $_{56}$.

Hygd.—Wife of Higelac, and daughter of Hæreth. There are some indications that she married Beowulf after she became a widow.— 28 $_{37}$.

Ingeld.—Son of the Heathobard king, Froda. Marries Hrothgar's daughter, Freaware, in order to reconcile the two peoples.—29 $_{62}$; 30 $_{32}$.

Ingwins.—Another name for the Danes.—16 $_{52}$; 20 $_{69}$.

Jutes.—Name sometimes applied to Finn's people.—17 $_{22}$; 17 $_{38}$; 18 $_{17}$.

Lafing.—Name of a famous sword presented to Hengest by Hun.—18 $_{19}$.

Merewing.—A Frankish king, probably engaged in the war in which Higelac was slain.—40 $_{29}$.

Nægling.—Beowulf's sword.—36 $_{76}$.

Offa.—King of the Angles, and son of Garmund. Marries the terrible Thrytho who is so strongly contrasted with Hygd.—28 $_{59}$; 28 $_{66}$.

Ohthere.—Son of Ongentheow, king of the Swedes. He is father of Eanmund and Eadgils.—40 $_{35}$; 40 $_{39}$.

Onela.—Brother of Ohthere.—36 $_{15}$; 40 $_{39}$.

Ongentheow.—King of Sweden, of the Scylfing dynasty. Married, perhaps, Elan, daughter of Healfdene.—35_{26}; 41_{16}.

Oslaf.—A Dane of Hnæf's party.—18_{24}.

Ravenswood.—The forest near which Hæthcyn was slain.—40_{31}; 40_{41}.

Scefing.—Applied (1 4) to Scyld, and meaning 'son of Scef.'

Scyld.—Founder of the dynasty to which Hrothgar, his father, and grandfather belonged. He dies, and his body is put on a vessel, and set adrift. He goes from Daneland just as he had come to it—in a bark.—1_4; 1_{19}; 1_{27}.

Scyldings.—The descendants of Scyld. They are also called Honor-Scyldings, Victory-Scyldings, War-Scyldings, etc. (See 'Danes,' above.)—2_1; 7_1; 8_1.

Scylfings.—A Swedish royal line to which Wiglaf belonged.—36_2.

Sigemund.—Son of Wæls, and uncle and father of Fitela. His struggle with a dragon is related in connection with Beowulf's deeds of prowess.—14_{38}; 14_{47}.

Swerting.—Grandfather of Higelac, and father of Hrethel.—19_{11}.

Swedes.—People of Sweden, ruled by the Scylfings.—35_{13}.

Thrytho.—Wife of Offa, king of the Angles. Known for her fierce and unwomanly disposition. She is introduced as a contrast to the gentle Hygd, queen of Higelac.—28_{42}; 28_{56}.

Unferth.—Son of Ecglaf, and seemingly a confidential courtier of Hrothgar. Taunts Beowulf for having taken part in the swimming-match. Lends Beowulf his sword when he goes to look for Grendel's mother. In the MS. sometimes written Hunferth. 9_1; 18_{41}.

Wæls.—Father of Sigemund.—14_{60}.

Wægmunding.—A name occasionally applied to Wiglaf and Beowulf, and perhaps derived from a common ancestor, Wægmund.—36_6; 38_{61}.

Weders.—Another name for Geats or Wedergeats.

Wayland.—A fabulous smith mentioned in this poem and in other old Teutonic literature.—7_{83}.

Wendels.—The people of Wulfgar, Hrothgar's messenger and retainer. (Perhaps = Vandals.)—6_{30}.

Wealhtheow.—Wife of Hrothgar. Her queenly courtesy is well shown in the poem.—10_{55}.

Weohstan, or Wihstan.—A Wægmunding, and father of Wiglaf.—36_1.

Whale's Ness.—A prominent promontory, on which Beowulf's mound was built.—38_{52}; 42_{76}.

Wiglaf.—Son of Wihstan, and related to Beowulf. He remains faithful to Beowulf in the fatal struggle with the fire-drake. Would rather die than leave his lord in his dire emergency.—36_1; 36_3; 36_{28}.

Wonred.—Father of Wulf and Eofor.—41 $_{20}$; 41 $_{26}$.

Wulf.—Son of Wonred. Engaged in the battle between Higelac's and Ongentheow's forces, and had a hand-to-hand fight with Ongentheow himself. Ongentheow disables him, and is thereupon slain by Eofor.—41 $_{19}$; 41 $_{29}$.

Wulfgar.—Lord of the Wendels, and retainer of Hrothgar.—6 $_{18}$; 6 $_{30}$.

Wylfings.—A people to whom belonged Heatholaf, who was slain by Ecgtheow.—8 $_{6}$; 8 $_{16}$.

Yrmenlaf.—Younger brother of Æschere, the hero whose death grieved Hrothgar so deeply.—21 $_{4}$.

List of Words and Phrases

NOT IN GENERAL USE.

ATHELING.—Prince, nobleman.
BAIRN.—Son, child.
BARROW.—Mound, rounded hill, funeral-mound.
BATTLE-SARK.—Armor.
BEAKER.—Cup, drinking-vessel.
BEGEAR.—Prepare.
BIGHT.—Bay, sea.
BILL.—Sword.
BOSS.—Ornamental projection.
BRACTEATE.—A round ornament on a necklace.
BRAND.—Sword.
BURN.—Stream.
BURNIE.—Armor.
CARLE.—Man, hero.
EARL.—Nobleman, any brave man.
EKE.—Also.
EMPRISE.—Enterprise, undertaking.
ERST.—Formerly.
ERST-WORTHY.—Worthy for a long time past.
FAIN.—Glad.
FERRY.—Bear, carry.
FEY.—Fated, doomed.
FLOAT.—Vessel, ship.
FOIN.—To lunge (Shaks.).
GLORY OF KINGS.—God.
GREWSOME.—Cruel, fierce.
HEFT.—Handle, hilt; used by synecdoche for 'sword.'
HELM.—Helmet, protector.
HENCHMAN.—Retainer, vassal.
HIGHT.—Am (was) named.
HOLM.—Ocean, curved surface of the sea.
HIMSEEMED.—(It) seemed to him.
LIEF.—Dear, valued.
MERE.—Sea; in compounds, 'mere-ways,' 'mere-currents,' etc.
MICKLE.—Much.
NATHLESS.—Nevertheless.
NAZE.—Edge (nose).
NESS.—Edge.
NICKER.—Sea-beast.
QUIT, QUITE.—Requite.

RATHE.—Quickly.
REAVE.—Bereave, deprive.
SAIL-ROAD.—Sea.
SETTLE.—Seat, bench.
SKINKER.—One who pours.
SOOTHLY.—Truly.
SWINGE.—Stroke, blow.
TARGE, TARGET.—Shield.
THROUGHLY.—Thoroughly.
TOLD.—Counted.
UNCANNY.—Ill-featured, grizzly.
UNNETHE.—Difficult.
WAR-SPEED.—Success in war.
WEB.—Tapestry (that which is 'woven').
WEEDED.—Clad (cf. widow's weeds).
WEEN.—Suppose, imagine.
WEIRD.—Fate, Providence.
WHILOM.—At times, formerly, often.
WIELDER.—Ruler. Often used of God; also in compounds, as 'Wielder
   of Glory,' 'Wielder of Worship.'
WIGHT.—Creature.
WOLD.—Plane, extended surface.
WOT.—Knows.
YOUNKER.—Youth.

Beowulf

I. The Life and Death of Scyld.

Lo! the Spear-Danes' glory through splendid achievements

[*The famous race of Spear-Danes.*][4]

The folk-kings' former fame we have heard of,
How princes displayed then their prowess-in-battle.
Oft Scyld the Scefing from scathers in numbers

> [*Scyld, their mighty king, in honor of whom they are often
> called Scyldings. He is the great-grandfather of Hrothgar,
> so prominent in the poem.*]

From many a people their mead-benches tore.
Since first he found him friendless and wretched,
The earl had had terror: comfort he got for it,
Waxed 'neath the welkin, world-honor gained,
Till all his neighbors o'er sea were compelled to
Bow to his bidding and bring him their tribute: 10
An excellent atheling! After was borne him
A son and heir, young in his dwelling,

> [*A son is born to him, who receives the name of Beowulf—a
> name afterwards made so famous by the hero of the
> poem.*]

Whom God-Father sent to solace the people.
He had marked the misery malice had caused them,
[5]That reaved of their rulers they wretched had erstwhile[6]
Long been afflicted. The Lord, in requital,
Wielder of Glory, with world-honor blessed him.
Famed was Beowulf, far spread the glory
Of Scyld's great son in the lands of the Danemen.
So the carle that is young, by kindnesses rendered   20
The friends of his father, with fees in abundance

---

[4] Notes in brackets correspond to side notes in original text.
[5] For the 'Þæt' of verse 15, Sievers suggests 'þá' (= which). If this be accepted, the sentence 'He had ... afflicted' will read: *He* (i.e. *God*) *had perceived the malice-caused sorrow which they, lordless, had formerly long endured.*
[6] For 'aldor-léase' (15) Gr. suggested 'aldor-ceare': *He perceived their distress, that they formerly had suffered life-sorrow a long while.*

[The ideal Teutonic king lavishes gifts on his vassals.]

Must be able to earn that when age approacheth
Eager companions aid him requitingly,
When war assaults him serve him as liegemen:
By praise-worthy actions must honor be got
'Mong all of the races. At the hour that was fated
Scyld then departed to the All-Father's keeping

[Scyld dies at the hour appointed by Fate.]

Warlike to wend him; away then they bare him
To the flood of the current, his fond-loving comrades,
As himself he had bidden, while the friend of the Scyldings   30
Word-sway wielded, and the well-lovèd land-prince
Long did rule them.[7] The ring-stemmèd vessel,
Bark of the atheling, lay there at anchor,
Icy in glimmer and eager for sailing;
The belovèd leader laid they down there,

[By his own request, his body is laid on a vessel and wafted
seaward.]

Giver of rings, on the breast of the vessel,
The famed by the mainmast. A many of jewels,
Of fretted embossings, from far-lands brought over,
Was placed near at hand then; and heard I not ever
That a folk ever furnished a float more superbly   40
With weapons of warfare, weeds for the battle,
Bills and burnies; on his bosom sparkled
Many a jewel that with him must travel
On the flush of the flood afar on the current.
And favors no fewer they furnished him soothly,
Excellent folk-gems, than others had given him
Who when first he was born outward did send him

[He leaves Daneland on the breast of a bark.]

---

[7] A very difficult passage. 'Áhte' (31) has no object. H. supplies 'geweald' from the context; and our translation is based upon this assumption, though it is far from satisfactory. Kl. suggests 'lændagas' for 'lange': *And the beloved land-prince enjoyed (had) his transitory days (i.e. lived)*. B. suggests a dislocation; but this is a dangerous doctrine, pushed rather far by that eminent scholar.

Lone on the main, the merest of infants:
And a gold-fashioned standard they stretched under heaven
High o'er his head, let the holm-currents bear him,   50
Seaward consigned him: sad was their spirit,
Their mood very mournful. Men are not able
Soothly to tell us, they in halls who reside,[8]

[*No one knows whither the boat drifted.*]

Heroes under heaven, to what haven he hied.

II. Scyld's Successors.—Hrothgar's Great Mead-Hall.

In the boroughs then Beowulf, bairn of the Scyldings,
Belovèd land-prince, for long-lasting season

[*Beowulf succeeds his father Scyld.*]

Was famed mid the folk (his father departed,
The prince from his dwelling), till afterward sprang
Great-minded Healfdene; the Danes in his lifetime
He graciously governed, grim-mooded, agèd.

[*Healfdene's birth.*]

Four bairns of his body born in succession
Woke in the world, war-troopers' leader
Heorogar, Hrothgar, and Halga the good;
Heard I that Elan was Ongentheow's consort,   10

[*He has three sons—one of them, Hrothgar—and a daughter
named Elan. Hrothgar becomes a mighty king.*]

The well-beloved bedmate of the War-Scylfing leader.
Then glory in battle to Hrothgar was given,
Waxing of war-fame, that willingly kinsmen
Obeyed his bidding, till the boys grew to manhood,
A numerous band. It burned in his spirit
To urge his folk to found a great building,
A mead-hall grander than men of the era

---

[8] The reading of the H.-So. text has been quite closely followed; but some eminent scholars read 'séle-rædenne' for 'sele-rædende.' If that be adopted, the passage will read: *Men cannot tell us, indeed, the order of Fate, etc.* 'Sele-rædende' has two things to support it: (1) v. 1347; (2) it affords a parallel to 'men' in v. 50.

[*He is eager to build a great hall in which he may feast his retainers.*]

Ever had heard of, and in it to share
With young and old all of the blessings
The Lord had allowed him, save life and retainers.   20
Then the work I find afar was assigned
To many races in middle-earth's regions,
To adorn the great folk-hall. In due time it happened
Early 'mong men, that 'twas finished entirely,
The greatest of hall-buildings; Heorot he named it

[*The hall is completed, and is called Heort, or Heorot.*]

Who wide-reaching word-sway wielded 'mong earlmen.
His promise he brake not, rings he lavished,
Treasure at banquet. Towered the hall up
High and horn-crested, huge between antlers:
It battle-waves bided, the blasting fire-demon;   30
Ere long then from hottest hatred must sword-wrath
Arise for a woman's husband and father.
Then the mighty war-spirit[9] endured for a season,

[*The Monster Grendel is madly envious of the Danemen's joy.*]

Bore it bitterly, he who bided in darkness,
That light-hearted laughter loud in the building
Greeted him daily; there was dulcet harp-music,
Clear song of the singer. He said that was able

[*The course of the story is interrupted by a short reference to some old account of the creation.*]

To tell from of old earthmen's beginnings,
That Father Almighty earth had created,
The winsome wold that the water encircleth,   40
Set exultingly the sun's and the moon's beams
To lavish their lustre on land-folk and races,
And earth He embellished in all her regions
With limbs and leaves; life He bestowed too

---

[9] R. and t. B. prefer 'ellor-gæst' to 'ellen-gæst' (86): *Then the stranger from afar endured, etc.*

On all the kindreds that live under heaven.
So blessed with abundance, brimming with joyance,

[*The glee of the warriors is overcast by a horrible dread.*]

The warriors abided, till a certain one gan to
Dog them with deeds of direfullest malice,
A foe in the hall-building: this horrible stranger[10]
Was Grendel entitled, the march-stepper famous   50
Who[11] dwelt in the moor-fens, the marsh and the fastness;
The wan-mooded being abode for a season
In the land of the giants, when the Lord and Creator
Had banned him and branded. For that bitter murder,
The killing of Abel, all-ruling Father
The kindred of Cain crushed with His vengeance;

[*Cain is referred to as a progenitor of Grendel, and of monsters in general.*]

In the feud He rejoiced not, but far away drove him
From kindred and kind, that crime to atone for,
Meter of Justice. Thence ill-favored creatures,
Elves and giants, monsters of ocean,   60
Came into being, and the giants that longtime
Grappled with God; He gave them requital.

III. Grendel the Murderer.

When the sun was sunken, he set out to visit

[*Grendel attacks the sleeping heroes.*]

The lofty hall-building, how the Ring-Danes had used it
For beds and benches when the banquet was over.
Then he found there reposing many a noble
Asleep after supper; sorrow the heroes,[12]
Misery knew not. The monster of evil
Greedy and cruel tarried but little,

---

[10] Some authorities would translate '*demon*' instead of '*stranger.*'

[11] Some authorities arrange differently, and render: *Who dwelt in the moor-fens, the marsh and the fastness, the land of the giant-race.*

[12] The translation is based on 'weras,' adopted by H.-So.—K. and Th. read 'wera' and, arranging differently, render 119(2)-120: *They knew not sorrow, the wretchedness of man, aught of misfortune.*—For 'unhælo' (120) R. suggests 'unfælo': The uncanny creature, greedy and cruel, etc.

Fell and frantic, and forced from their slumbers

[*He drags off thirty of them, and devours them.*]

Thirty of thanemen; thence he departed
Leaping and laughing, his lair to return to,   10
With surfeit of slaughter sallying homeward.
In the dusk of the dawning, as the day was just breaking,
Was Grendel's prowess revealed to the warriors:
Then, his meal-taking finished, a moan was uplifted,

[*A cry of agony goes up, when Grendel's horrible deed is fully realized.*]

Morning-cry mighty. The man-ruler famous,
The long-worthy atheling, sat very woful,
Suffered great sorrow, sighed for his liegemen,
When they had seen the track of the hateful pursuer,
The spirit accursèd: too crushing that sorrow,
Too loathsome and lasting. Not longer he tarried,   20

[*The monster returns the next night.*]

But one night after continued his slaughter
Shameless and shocking, shrinking but little
From malice and murder; they mastered him fully.
He was easy to find then who otherwhere looked for
A pleasanter place of repose in the lodges,
A bed in the bowers. Then was brought to his notice
Told him truly by token apparent
The hall-thane's hatred: he held himself after
Further and faster who the foeman did baffle.
[13]So ruled he and strongly strove against justice   30
Lone against all men, till empty uptowered
The choicest of houses. Long was the season:

[*King Hrothgar's agony and suspense last twelve years.*]

Twelve-winters' time torture suffered
The friend of the Scyldings, every affliction,
Endless agony; hence it after[14] became

---

[13] S. rearranges and translates: *So he ruled and struggled unjustly, one against all, till the noblest of buildings stood useless (it was a long while) twelve years' time: the friend of the Scyldings suffered distress, every woe, great sorrows, etc.*

Certainly known to the children of men
Sadly in measures, that long against Hrothgar
Grendel struggled:—his grudges he cherished,
Murderous malice, many a winter,
Strife unremitting, and peacefully wished he   40
[15]Life-woe to lift from no liegeman at all of
The men of the Dane-folk, for money to settle,
No counsellor needed count for a moment
On handsome amends at the hands of the murderer;
The monster of evil fiercely did harass,

[*Grendel is unremitting in his persecutions.*]

The ill-planning death-shade, both elder and younger,
Trapping and tricking them. He trod every night then
The mist-covered moor-fens; men do not know where
Witches and wizards wander and ramble.
So the foe of mankind many of evils   50
Grievous injuries, often accomplished,
Horrible hermit; Heort he frequented,
Gem-bedecked palace, when night-shades had fallen
(Since God did oppose him, not the throne could he touch,[16]

[*God is against the monster.*]

The light-flashing jewel, love of Him knew not).
'Twas a fearful affliction to the friend of the Scyldings
Soul-crushing sorrow. Not seldom in private

[*The king and his council deliberate in vain.*]

---

[14] For 'syðð̄an,' B. suggests 'sárcwidum': *Hence in mournful words it became well known, etc.* Various other words beginning with 's' have been conjectured.

[15] The H.-So. glossary is very inconsistent in referring to this passage.—'Sibbe' (154), which H.-So. regards as an instr., B. takes as accus., obj. of 'wolde.' Putting a comma after Deniga, he renders: *He did not desire peace with any of the Danes, nor did he wish to remove their life-woe, nor to settle for money.*

[16] Of this difficult passage the following interpretations among others are given: (1) Though Grendel has frequented Heorot as a demon, he could not become ruler of the Danes, on account of his hostility to God. (2) Hrothgar was much grieved that Grendel had not appeared before his throne to receive presents. (3) He was not permitted to devastate the hall, on account of the Creator; *i.e.* God wished to make his visit fatal to him.—Ne ... wisse (169) W. renders: *Nor had he any desire to do so*; 'his' being obj. gen. = danach.

Sat the king in his council; conference held they
What the braves should determine 'gainst terrors unlooked for.
At the shrines of their idols often they promised   60

[*They invoke the aid of their gods.*]

Gifts and offerings, earnestly prayed they
The devil from hell would help them to lighten
Their people's oppression. Such practice they used then,
Hope of the heathen; hell they remembered
In innermost spirit, God they knew not,
Judge of their actions, All-wielding Ruler,

[*The true God they do not know.*]

No praise could they give the Guardian of Heaven,
The Wielder of Glory. Woe will be his who
Through furious hatred his spirit shall drive to
The clutch of the fire, no comfort shall look for,   70
Wax no wiser; well for the man who,
Living his life-days, his Lord may face
And find defence in his Father's embrace!

IV. Beowulf Goes to Hrothgar's Assistance.

So Healfdene's kinsman constantly mused on

[*Hrothgar sees no way of escape from the persecutions of
Grendel.*]

His long-lasting sorrow; the battle-thane clever
Was not anywise able evils to 'scape from:
Too crushing the sorrow that came to the people,
Loathsome and lasting the life-grinding torture,
Greatest of night-woes. So Higelac's liegeman,

[*Beowulf, the Geat, hero of the poem, hears of Hrothgar's
sorrow, and resolves to go to his assistance.*]

Good amid Geatmen, of Grendel's achievements
Heard in his home:[17] of heroes then living
He was stoutest and strongest, sturdy and noble.
He bade them prepare him a bark that was trusty;   10
He said he the war-king would seek o'er the ocean,
The folk-leader noble, since he needed retainers.
For the perilous project prudent companions
Chided him little, though loving him dearly;
They egged the brave atheling, augured him glory.
The excellent knight from the folk of the Geatmen

[*With fourteen carefully chosen companions, he sets out for
Dane-land.*]

Had liegemen selected, likest to prove them
Trustworthy warriors; with fourteen companions
The vessel he looked for; a liegeman then showed them,
A sea-crafty man, the bounds of the country.   20
Fast the days fleeted; the float was a-water,
The craft by the cliff. Clomb to the prow then
Well-equipped warriors: the wave-currents twisted
The sea on the sand; soldiers then carried
On the breast of the vessel bright-shining jewels,
Handsome war-armor; heroes outshoved then,
Warmen the wood-ship, on its wished-for adventure.
The foamy-necked floater fanned by the breeze,

[*The vessel sails like a bird.*]

Likest a bird, glided the waters,
Till twenty and four hours thereafter   30

[*In twenty four hours they reach the shores of Hrothgar's
dominions.*]

The twist-stemmed vessel had traveled such distance
That the sailing-men saw the sloping embankments,
The sea cliffs gleaming, precipitous mountains,
Nesses enormous: they were nearing the limits

---

[17] 'From hám' (194) is much disputed. One rendering is: *Beowulf, being away from
home, heard of Hrothgar's troubles, etc.* Another, that adopted by S. and endorsed in the
H.-So. notes, is: *B. heard from his neighborhood (neighbors),* i.e. *in his home, etc.* A
third is: *B., being at home, heard this as occurring away from home.* The H.-So. glossary
and notes conflict.

At the end of the ocean.[18] Up thence quickly
The men of the Weders clomb to the mainland,
Fastened their vessel (battle weeds rattled,
War burnies clattered), the Wielder they thanked
That the ways o'er the waters had waxen so gentle.
Then well from the cliff edge the guard of the Scyldings   40

[*They are hailed by the Danish coast guard.*]

Who the sea-cliffs should see to, saw o'er the gangway
Brave ones bearing beauteous targets,
Armor all ready, anxiously thought he,
Musing and wondering what men were approaching.
High on his horse then Hrothgar's retainer
Turned him to coastward, mightily brandished
His lance in his hands, questioned with boldness.
"Who are ye men here, mail-covered warriors

[*His challenge.*]

Clad in your corslets, come thus a-driving
A high riding ship o'er the shoals of the waters,   50
[19]And hither 'neath helmets have hied o'er the ocean?
I have been strand-guard, standing as warden,
Lest enemies ever anywise ravage
Danish dominions with army of war-ships.
More boldly never have warriors ventured
Hither to come; of kinsmen's approval,
Word-leave of warriors, I ween that ye surely
Nothing have known. Never a greater one

[*He is struck by Beowulf's appearance.*]

---

[18] 'Eoletes' (224) is marked with a (?) by H.-So.; our rendering simply follows his conjecture.—Other conjectures as to 'eolet' are: (1) *voyage*, (2) *toil, labor*, (3) *hasty journey*.

[19] The lacuna of the MS at this point has been supplied by various conjectures. The reading adopted by H.-So. has been rendered in the above translation. W., like H.-So., makes 'ic' the beginning of a new sentence, but, for 'helmas bæron,' he reads 'hringed stefnan.' This has the advantage of giving a parallel to 'brontne ceol' instead of a kenning for 'go.'—B puts the (?) after 'holmas', and begins a new sentence at the middle of the line. Translate: *What warriors are ye, clad in armor, who have thus come bringing the foaming vessel over the water way, hither over the seas? For some time on the wall I have been coast guard, etc.* S. endorses most of what B. says, but leaves out 'on the wall' in the last sentence. If W.'s 'hringed stefnan' be accepted, change line 51 above to, *A ring-stemmed vessel hither o'ersea.*

Of earls o'er the earth have *I* had a sight of
Than is one of your number, a hero in armor; 60
No low-ranking fellow[20] adorned with his weapons,
But launching them little, unless looks are deceiving,
And striking appearance. Ere ye pass on your journey
As treacherous spies to the land of the Scyldings
And farther fare, I fully must know now
What race ye belong to. Ye far-away dwellers,
Sea-faring sailors, my simple opinion
Hear ye and hearken: haste is most fitting
Plainly to tell me what place ye are come from."

V. The Geats Reach Heorot.

The chief of the strangers rendered him answer,

[*Beowulf courteously replies.*]

War-troopers' leader, and word-treasure opened:
"We are sprung from the lineage of the people of Geatland,

[*We are Geats.*]

And Higelac's hearth-friends. To heroes unnumbered
My father was known, a noble head-warrior

[*My father Ecgtheow was well-known in his day.*]

Ecgtheow titled; many a winter
He lived with the people, ere he passed on his journey,
Old from his dwelling; each of the counsellors
Widely mid world-folk well remembers him.
We, kindly of spirit, the lord of thy people, 10

[*Our intentions towards King Hrothgar are of the kindest.*]

The son of King Healfdene, have come here to visit,
Folk-troop's defender: be free in thy counsels!
To the noble one bear we a weighty commission,
The helm of the Danemen; we shall hide, I ween,
Naught of our message. Thou know'st if it happen,

---

[20] 'Seld-guma' (249) is variously rendered: (1) *housecarle*; (2) *home-stayer*; (3) *common man*. Dr. H. Wood suggests *a man-at-arms in another's house*.

[*Is it true that a monster is slaying Danish heroes?*]

As we soothly heard say, that some savage despoiler,
Some hidden pursuer, on nights that are murky
By deeds very direful 'mid the Danemen exhibits
Hatred unheard of, horrid destruction
And the falling of dead. From feelings least selfish   20
I am able to render counsel to Hrothgar,

[*I can help your king to free himself from this horrible
creature.*]

How he, wise and worthy, may worst the destroyer,
If the anguish of sorrow should ever be lessened,[21]
Comfort come to him, and care-waves grow cooler,
Or ever hereafter he agony suffer
And troublous distress, while towereth upward
The handsomest of houses high on the summit."
Bestriding his stallion, the strand-watchman answered,

[*The coast-guard reminds Beowulf that it is easier to say than
to do.*]

The doughty retainer: "The difference surely
'Twixt words and works, the warlike shield-bearer   30
Who judgeth wisely well shall determine.
This band, I hear, beareth no malice
To the prince of the Scyldings. Pass ye then onward

[*I am satisfied of your good intentions, and shall lead you to
the palace.*]

With weapons and armor. I shall lead you in person;
To my war-trusty vassals command I shall issue
To keep from all injury your excellent vessel,

[*Your boat shall be well cared for during your stay here.*]

---

[21] 'Edwendan' (280) B. takes to be the subs. 'edwenden' (cf. 1775); and 'bisigu' he
takes as gen. sing., limiting 'edwenden': *If reparation for sorrows is ever to come.* This is
supported by t. B.

Your fresh-tarred craft, 'gainst every opposer
Close by the sea-shore, till the curvèd-neckèd bark shall
Waft back again the well-beloved hero
O'er the way of the water to Weder dominions.   40
To warrior so great 'twill be granted sure

[*He again compliments Beowulf.*]

In the storm of strife to stand secure."
Onward they fared then (the vessel lay quiet,
The broad-bosomed bark was bound by its cable,
Firmly at anchor); the boar-signs glistened[22]
Bright on the visors vivid with gilding,
Blaze-hardened, brilliant; the boar acted warden.
The heroes hastened, hurried the liegemen,
Descended together, till they saw the great palace,

[*The land is perhaps rolling.*]

The well-fashioned wassail-hall wondrous and gleaming: 50
'Mid world-folk and kindreds that was widest reputed

[*Heorot flashes on their view.*]

Of halls under heaven which the hero abode in;
Its lustre enlightened lands without number.
Then the battle-brave hero showed them the glittering
Court of the bold ones, that they easily thither
Might fare on their journey; the aforementioned warrior
Turning his courser, quoth as he left them:
"'Tis time I were faring; Father Almighty

[*The coast-guard, having discharged his duty, bids them God-speed.*]

Grant you His grace, and give you to journey
Safe on your mission! To the sea I will get me   60
'Gainst hostile warriors as warden to stand."

---

[22] Combining the emendations of B. and t. B., we may read: *The boar-images glistened ... brilliant, protected the life of the war-mooded man.* They read 'ferh-wearde' (305) and 'gúðmódgum men' (306).

VI. Beowulf Introduces Himself at the Palace.

The highway glistened with many-hued pebble,
A by-path led the liegemen together.
[23]Firm and hand-locked the war-burnie glistened,
The ring-sword radiant rang 'mid the armor
As the party was approaching the palace together

[*They set their arms and armor against the wall.*]

In warlike equipments. 'Gainst the wall of the building
Their wide-fashioned war-shields they weary did set then,
Battle-shields sturdy; benchward they turned then;
Their battle-sarks rattled, the gear of the heroes;
The lances stood up then, all in a cluster,   10
The arms of the seamen, ashen-shafts mounted
With edges of iron: the armor-clad troopers
Were decked with weapons. Then a proud-mooded hero

[*A Danish hero asks them whence and why they are come.*]

Asked of the champions questions of lineage:
"From what borders bear ye your battle-shields plated,
Gilded and gleaming, your gray-colored burnies,
Helmets with visors and heap of war-lances?—
To Hrothgar the king I am servant and liegeman.
'Mong folk from far-lands found I have never
Men so many of mien more courageous.   20

[*He expresses no little admiration for the strangers.*]

I ween that from valor, nowise as outlaws,
But from greatness of soul ye sought for King Hrothgar."
Then the strength-famous earlman answer rendered,

[*Beowulf replies.*]

The proud-mooded Wederchief replied to his question,
Hardy 'neath helmet: "Higelac's mates are we;

---

[23] Instead of the punctuation given by H.-So, S. proposed to insert a comma after
'scír' (322), and to take 'hring-íren' as meaning 'ring-mail' and as parallel with 'gúð-
byrne.' The passage would then read: *The firm and hand-locked war-burnie shone, bright
ring-mail, rang 'mid the armor, etc.*

[We are Higelac's table-companions, and bear an important
commission to your prince.]

Beowulf hight I. To the bairn of Healfdene,
The famous folk-leader, I freely will tell
To thy prince my commission, if pleasantly hearing
He'll grant we may greet him so gracious to all men."
Wulfgar replied then (he was prince of the Wendels,   30
His boldness of spirit was known unto many,
His prowess and prudence): "The prince of the Scyldings,
The friend-lord of Danemen, I will ask of thy journey,

[Wulfgar, the thane, says that he will go and ask Hrothgar
whether he will see the strangers.]

The giver of rings, as thou urgest me do it,
The folk-chief famous, and inform thee early
What answer the good one mindeth to render me."
He turned then hurriedly where Hrothgar was sitting,
[24]Old and hoary, his earlmen attending him;
The strength-famous went till he stood at the shoulder
Of the lord of the Danemen, of courteous thanemen   40
The custom he minded. Wulfgar addressed then
His friendly liegelord: "Folk of the Geatmen
O'er the way of the waters are wafted hither,

[He thereupon urges his liegelord to receive the visitors
courteously.]

Faring from far-lands: the foremost in rank
The battle-champions Beowulf title.
They make this petition: with thee, O my chieftain,
To be granted a conference; O gracious King Hrothgar,
Friendly answer refuse not to give them!
In war-trappings weeded worthy they seem

[Hrothgar, too, is struck with Beowulf's appearance.]

Of earls to be honored; sure the atheling is doughty   50
Who headed the heroes hitherward coming."

---

[24] Gr. and others translate 'unhár' by 'bald'; *old and bald.*

VII. Hrothgar and Beowulf.

Hrothgar answered, helm of the Scyldings:

[*Hrothgar remembers Beowulf as a youth, and also remembers his father.*]

"I remember this man as the merest of striplings.
His father long dead now was Ecgtheow titled,
Him Hrethel the Geatman granted at home his
One only daughter; his battle-brave son
Is come but now, sought a trustworthy friend.
Seafaring sailors asserted it then,
Who valuable gift-gems of the Geatmen[25] carried

[*Beowulf is reported to have the strength of thirty men.*]

As peace-offering thither, that he thirty men's grapple
Has in his hand, the hero-in-battle.   10
The holy Creator usward sent him,

[*God hath sent him to our rescue.*]

To West-Dane warriors, I ween, for to render
'Gainst Grendel's grimness gracious assistance:
I shall give to the good one gift-gems for courage.
Hasten to bid them hither to speed them,[26]
To see assembled this circle of kinsmen;
Tell them expressly they're welcome in sooth to
The men of the Danes." To the door of the building
Wulfgar went then, this word-message shouted:

[*Wulfgar invites the strangers in.*]

"My victorious liegelord bade me to tell you,   20
The East-Danes' atheling, that your origin knows he,
And o'er wave-billows wafted ye welcome are hither,
Valiant of spirit. Ye straightway may enter
Clad in corslets, cased in your helmets,
To see King Hrothgar. Here let your battle-boards,

---

[25] Some render 'gif-sceattas' by 'tribute.'—'Géata' B. and Th. emended to 'Géatum.' If this be accepted, change '*of* the Geatmen' to '*to* the Geatmen.'

[26] If t. B.'s emendation of vv. 386, 387 be accepted, the two lines, 'Hasten ... kinsmen' will read: *Hasten thou, bid the throng of kinsmen go into the hall together.*

Wood-spears and war-shafts, await your conferring."
The mighty one rose then, with many a liegeman,
An excellent thane-group; some there did await them,
And as bid of the brave one the battle-gear guarded.
Together they hied them, while the hero did guide them,   30
'Neath Heorot's roof; the high-minded went then
Sturdy 'neath helmet till he stood in the building.
Beowulf spake (his burnie did glisten,
His armor seamed over by the art of the craftsman):
"Hail thou, Hrothgar! I am Higelac's kinsman

[*Beowulf salutes Hrothgar, and then proceeds to boast of his youthful achievements.*]

And vassal forsooth; many a wonder
I dared as a stripling. The doings of Grendel,
In far-off fatherland I fully did know of:
Sea-farers tell us, this hall-building standeth,
Excellent edifice, empty and useless   40
To all the earlmen after evenlight's glimmer
'Neath heaven's bright hues hath hidden its glory.
This my earls then urged me, the most excellent of them,
Carles very clever, to come and assist thee,
Folk-leader Hrothgar; fully they knew of
The strength of my body. Themselves they beheld me

[*His fight with the nickers.*]

When I came from the contest, when covered with gore
Foes I escaped from, where five[27] I had bound,
The giant-race wasted, in the waters destroying
The nickers by night, bore numberless sorrows,   50
The Weders avenged (woes had they suffered)
Enemies ravaged; alone now with Grendel
I shall manage the matter, with the monster of evil,

[*He intends to fight Grendel unaided.*]

---

[27] For 420 (*b*) and 421 (*a*), B. suggests: Þær ic (on) fífelgeban ýðde eotena cyn = *where I in the ocean destroyed the eoten-race.*—t. B. accepts B.'s "brilliant" 'fífelgeban,' omits 'on,' emends 'cyn' to 'hám,' arranging: Þær ic fifelgeban ýðde, eotena hám = *where I desolated the ocean, the home of the eotens.*—This would be better but for changing 'cyn' to 'hám.'—I suggest: Þær ic fifelgeband (cf. nhd. Bande) ýðde, eotena cyn = *where I conquered the monster band, the race of the eotens.* This makes no change except to read 'fifel' for 'fife.'

The giant, decide it. Thee I would therefore
Beg of thy bounty, Bright-Danish chieftain,
Lord of the Scyldings, this single petition:
Not to refuse me, defender of warriors,
Friend-lord of folks, so far have I sought thee,
That *I* may unaided, my earlmen assisting me,
This brave-mooded war-band, purify Heorot.   60
I have heard on inquiry, the horrible creature
From veriest rashness recks not for weapons;

[*Since the monster uses no weapons,*]

I this do scorn then, so be Higelac gracious,
My liegelord belovèd, lenient of spirit,
To bear a blade or a broad-fashioned target,
A shield to the onset; only with hand-grip
The foe I must grapple, fight for my life then,

[*I, too, shall disdain to use any.*]

Foeman with foeman; he fain must rely on
The doom of the Lord whom death layeth hold of.
I ween he will wish, if he win in the struggle,   70

[*Should he crush me, he will eat my companions as he has
eaten thy thanes.*]

To eat in the war-hall earls of the Geat-folk,
Boldly to swallow[28] them, as of yore he did often
The best of the Hrethmen! Thou needest not trouble
A head-watch to give me;[29] he will have me dripping
And dreary with gore, if death overtake me,[30]

---

[28] 'Unforhte' (444) is much disputed.—H.-So. wavers between adj. and adv. Gr. and
B. take it as an adv. modifying etan: *Will eat the Geats fearlessly.*—Kl. considers this
reading absurd, and proposes 'anforhte' = timid.—Understanding 'unforhte' as an adj.
has this advantage, viz. that it gives a parallel to 'Geátena leóde': but to take it as an adv.
is more natural. Furthermore, to call the Geats 'brave' might, at this point, seem like an
implied thrust at the Danes, so long helpless; while to call his own men 'timid' would be
befouling his own nest.

[29] For 'head-watch,' *cf.* H.-So. notes and *cf.* v. 2910.—Th. translates: *Thou wilt not
need my head to hide* (*i.e.*, thou wilt have no occasion to bury me, as Grendel will devour
me whole).—Simrock imagines a kind of dead-watch.—Dr. H. Wood suggests: *Thou wilt
not have to bury so much as my head* (for Grendel will be a thorough undertaker),—grim
humor.

[30] S. proposes a colon after 'nimeð' (l. 447). This would make no essential change
in the translation.

[*In case of my defeat, thou wilt not have the trouble of burying me.*]

Will bear me off bleeding, biting and mouthing me,
The hermit will eat me, heedless of pity,
Marking the moor-fens; no more wilt thou need then
Find me my food.[31] If I fall in the battle,

[*Should I fall, send my armor to my lord, King Higelac.*]

Send to Higelac the armor that serveth   80
To shield my bosom, the best of equipments,
Richest of ring-mails; 'tis the relic of Hrethla,
The work of Wayland. Goes Weird as she must go!"

[*Weird is supreme.*]

VIII. Hrothgar And Beowulf.—Continued.

Hrothgar discoursed, helm of the Scyldings:

[*Hrothgar responds.*]

"To defend our folk and to furnish assistance,[32]
Thou soughtest us hither, good friend Beowulf.
The fiercest of feuds thy father engaged in,

[*Reminiscences of Beowulf's father, Ecgtheow.*]

Heatholaf killed he in hand-to-hand conflict
'Mid Wilfingish warriors; then the Wederish people
For fear of a feud were forced to disown him.
Thence flying he fled to the folk of the South-Danes,

---

[31] Owing to the vagueness of 'feorme' (451), this passage is variously translated. In our translation, H.-So.'s glossary has been quite closely followed. This agrees substantially with B.'s translation (P. and B. XII. 87). R. translates: *Thou needst not take care longer as to the consumption of my dead body.* 'Líc' is also a crux here, as it may mean living body or dead body.

[32] B. and S. reject the reading given in H.-So., and suggested by Grtvg. B. suggests for 457-458:

wáere-ryhtum Þú, wine mín Béowulf,
and for ár-stafum úsic sóhtest.

This means: *From the obligations of clientage, my friend Beowulf, and for assistance thou hast sought us.*—This gives coherence to Hrothgar's opening remarks in VIII., and also introduces a new motive for Beowulf's coming to Hrothgar's aid.

The race of the Scyldings, o'er the roll of the waters;
I had lately begun then to govern the Danemen,   10
The hoard-seat of heroes held in my youth,
Rich in its jewels: dead was Heregar,
My kinsman and elder had earth-joys forsaken,
Healfdene his bairn. He was better than I am!
That feud thereafter for a fee I compounded;
O'er the weltering waters to the Wilfings I sent
Ornaments old; oaths did he swear me.

> [*Hrothgar recounts to Beowulf the horrors of Grendel's persecutions.*]

It pains me in spirit to any to tell it,
What grief in Heorot Grendel hath caused me,
What horror unlooked-for, by hatred unceasing.   20
Waned is my war-band, wasted my hall-troop;
Weird hath offcast them to the clutches of Grendel.
God can easily hinder the scather
From deeds so direful. Oft drunken with beer
O'er the ale-vessel promised warriors in armor

> [*My thanes have made many boasts, but have not executed them.*]

They would willingly wait on the wassailing-benches
A grapple with Grendel, with grimmest of edges.
Then this mead-hall at morning with murder was reeking,
The building was bloody at breaking of daylight,
The bench-deals all flooded, dripping and bloodied,   30
The folk-hall was gory: I had fewer retainers,
Dear-beloved warriors, whom death had laid hold of.
Sit at the feast now, thy intents unto heroes,[33]

> [*Sit down to the feast, and give us comfort.*]

Thy victor-fame show, as thy spirit doth urge thee!"
For the men of the Geats then together assembled,

---

[33] *Sit now at the feast, and disclose thy purposes to the victorious heroes, as thy spirit urges.*—Kl. reaches the above translation by erasing the comma after 'meoto' and reading 'sige-hrèðsecgum.'—There are other and bolder emendations and suggestions. Of these the boldest is to regard 'meoto' as a verb (imperative), and read 'on sǽl': *Think upon gayety, etc.*—All the renderings are unsatisfactory, the one given in our translation involving a zeugma.

[*A bench is made ready for Beowulf and his party.*]

In the beer-hall blithesome a bench was made ready;
There warlike in spirit they went to be seated,
Proud and exultant. A liegeman did service,
Who a beaker embellished bore with decorum,
And gleaming-drink poured. The gleeman sang whilom   40

[*The gleeman sings.*]

Hearty in Heorot; there was heroes' rejoicing,

[*The heroes all rejoice together.*]

A numerous war-band of Weders and Danemen.

IX. Unferth Taunts Beowulf.

Unferth spoke up, Ecglaf his son,

[*Unferth, a thane of Hrothgar, is jealous of Beowulf, and
undertakes to twit him.*]

Who sat at the feet of the lord of the Scyldings,
Opened the jousting (the journey[34] of Beowulf,
Sea-farer doughty, gave sorrow to Unferth
And greatest chagrin, too, for granted he never
That any man else on earth should attain to,
Gain under heaven, more glory than he):
"Art thou that Beowulf with Breca did struggle,

[*Did you take part in a swimming-match with Breca?*]

On the wide sea-currents at swimming contended,
Where to humor your pride the ocean ye tried,   10
From vainest vaunting adventured your bodies

[*'Twas mere folly that actuated you both to risk your lives on
the ocean.*]

---

[34] It has been plausibly suggested that 'síð' (in 501 and in 353) means 'arrival.' If
so, translate the bracket: (*the arrival of Beowulf, the brave seafarer, was a source of
great chagrin to Unferth, etc.*).

In care of the waters? And no one was able
Nor lief nor loth one, in the least to dissuade you
Your difficult voyage; then ye ventured a-swimming,
Where your arms outstretching the streams ye did cover,
The mere-ways measured, mixing and stirring them,
Glided the ocean; angry the waves were,
With the weltering of winter. In the water's possession,
Ye toiled for a seven-night; he at swimming outdid thee,
In strength excelled thee. Then early at morning   20
On the Heathoremes' shore the holm-currents tossed him,
Sought he thenceward the home of his fathers,
Beloved of his liegemen, the land of the Brondings,
The peace-castle pleasant, where a people he wielded,
Had borough and jewels. The pledge that he made thee
The son of Beanstan hath soothly accomplished.

> [*Breca outdid you entirely.*]

Then I ween thou wilt find thee less fortunate issue,
Though ever triumphant in onset of battle,

> [*Much more will Grendel outdo you, if you vie with him in
> prowess.*]

A grim grappling, if Grendel thou darest
For the space of a night near-by to wait for!"   30
Beowulf answered, offspring of Ecgtheow:

> [*Beowulf retaliates.*]

"My good friend Unferth, sure freely and wildly,
Thou fuddled with beer of Breca hast spoken,

> [*O friend Unferth, you are fuddled with beer, and cannot talk
> coherently.*]

Hast told of his journey! A fact I allege it,
That greater strength in the waters I had then,
Ills in the ocean, than any man else had.
We made agreement as the merest of striplings
Promised each other (both of us then were
Younkers in years) that we yet would adventure

> [*We simply kept an engagement made in early life.*]

Out on the ocean; it all we accomplished.   40
While swimming the sea-floods, sword-blade unscabbarded
Boldly we brandished, our bodies expected
To shield from the sharks. He sure was unable
To swim on the waters further than I could,

[*He* could *not excel me, and I* would *not excel him.*]

More swift on the waves, nor *would* I from him go.
Then we two companions stayed in the ocean
Five nights together, till the currents did part us,

[*After five days the currents separated us.*]

The weltering waters, weathers the bleakest,
And nethermost night, and the north-wind whistled
Fierce in our faces; fell were the billows.   50
The mere fishes' mood was mightily ruffled:
And there against foemen my firm-knotted corslet,
Hand-jointed, hardy, help did afford me;
My battle-sark braided, brilliantly gilded,
Lay on my bosom. To the bottom then dragged me,

[*A horrible sea-beast attacked me, but I slew him.*]

A hateful fiend-scather, seized me and held me,
Grim in his grapple: 'twas granted me, nathless,
To pierce the monster with the point of my weapon,
My obedient blade; battle offcarried
The mighty mere-creature by means of my hand-blow.   60

X. Beowulf Silences Unferth.—Glee Is High.

"So ill-meaning enemies often did cause me
Sorrow the sorest. I served them, in quittance,
With my dear-lovèd sword, as in sooth it was fitting;

[*My dear sword always served me faithfully.*]

They missed the pleasure of feasting abundantly,
Ill-doers evil, of eating my body,
Of surrounding the banquet deep in the ocean;
But wounded with edges early at morning
They were stretched a-high on the strand of the ocean,

Put to sleep with the sword, that sea-going travelers

[*I put a stop to the outrages of the sea-monsters.*]

No longer thereafter were hindered from sailing   10
The foam-dashing currents. Came a light from the east,
God's beautiful beacon; the billows subsided,
That well I could see the nesses projecting,
The blustering crags. Weird often saveth

[*Fortune helps the brave earl.*]

The undoomed hero if doughty his valor!
But me did it fortune[35] to fell with my weapon
Nine of the nickers. Of night-struggle harder
'Neath dome of the heaven heard I but rarely,
Nor of wight more woful in the waves of the ocean;
Yet I 'scaped with my life the grip of the monsters,   20
Weary from travel. Then the waters bare me

[*After that escape I drifted to Finland.*]

To the land of the Finns, the flood with the current,
The weltering waves. Not a word hath been told me

[*I have never heard of your doing any such bold deeds.*]

Of deeds so daring done by thee, Unferth,
And of sword-terror none; never hath Breca
At the play of the battle, nor either of you two,
Feat so fearless performèd with weapons
Glinting and gleaming . . . .
. . . . I utter no boasting;
Though with cold-blooded cruelty thou killedst thy brothers,   30

[*You are a slayer of brothers, and will suffer damnation, wise*
as you may be.]

Thy nearest of kin; thou needs must in hell get
Direful damnation, though doughty thy wisdom.
I tell thee in earnest, offspring of Ecglaf,

---

[35] The repetition of 'hwæðere' (574 and 578) is regarded by some scholars as a
defect. B. suggests 'swá Þær' for the first: So there it befell me, etc. Another suggestion
is to change the second 'hwæðere' into 'swá Þær': *So there I escaped with my life, etc.*

Never had Grendel such numberless horrors,
The direful demon, done to thy liegelord,
Harrying in Heorot, if thy heart were as sturdy,
Thy mood as ferocious as thou dost describe them.

[*Had your acts been as brave as your words, Grendel had not*
    ravaged your land so long.]

He hath found out fully that the fierce-burning hatred,
The edge-battle eager, of all of your kindred,
Of the Victory-Scyldings, need little dismay him: 40
Oaths he exacteth, not any he spares
Of the folk of the Danemen, but fighteth with pleasure,

[*The monster is not afraid of the Danes,*

Killeth and feasteth, no contest expecteth
From Spear-Danish people. But the prowess and valor

    but he will soon learn to dread the Geats.]

Of the earls of the Geatmen early shall venture
To give him a grapple. He shall go who is able
Bravely to banquet, when the bright-light of morning
Which the second day bringeth, the sun in its ether-robes,

[*On the second day, any warrior may go unmolested to the*
    mead-banquet.]

O'er children of men shines from the southward!"
Then the gray-haired, war-famed giver of treasure   50
Was blithesome and joyous, the Bright-Danish ruler

[*Hrothgar's spirits are revived.*]

Expected assistance; the people's protector
Heard from Beowulf his bold resolution.

[*The old king trusts Beowulf. The heroes are joyful.*]

There was laughter of heroes; loud was the clatter,
The words were winsome. Wealhtheow advanced then,
Consort of Hrothgar, of courtesy mindful,

[*Queen Wealhtheow plays the hostess.*]

Gold-decked saluted the men in the building,
And the freeborn woman the beaker presented
To the lord of the kingdom, first of the East-Danes,

[*She offers the cup to her husband first.*]

Bade him be blithesome when beer was a-flowing,   60
Lief to his liegemen; he lustily tasted
Of banquet and beaker, battle-famed ruler.
The Helmingish lady then graciously circled
'Mid all the liegemen lesser and greater:
Treasure-cups tendered, till time was afforded

[*She gives presents to the heroes.*]

That the decorous-mooded, diademed folk-queen
Might bear to Beowulf the bumper o'errunning;

[*Then she offers the cup to Beowulf, thanking God that aid has
come.*]

She greeted the Geat-prince, God she did thank,
Most wise in her words, that her wish was accomplished,
That in any of earlmen she ever should look for   70
Solace in sorrow. He accepted the beaker,
Battle-bold warrior, at Wealhtheow's giving,
Then equipped for combat quoth he in measures,

[*Beowulf states to the queen the object of his visit.*]

Beowulf spake, offspring of Ecgtheow:
"I purposed in spirit when I mounted the ocean,
When I boarded my boat with a band of my liegemen,

[*I determined to do or die.*]

I would work to the fullest the will of your people
Or in foe's-clutches fastened fall in the battle.
Deeds I shall do of daring and prowess,
Or the last of my life-days live in this mead-hall."   80
These words to the lady were welcome and pleasing,
The boast of the Geatman; with gold trappings broidered
Went the freeborn folk-queen her fond-lord to sit by.
Then again as of yore was heard in the building

[*Glee is high.*]

Courtly discussion, conquerors' shouting,
Heroes were happy, till Healfdene's son would
Go to his slumber to seek for refreshing;
For the horrid hell-monster in the hall-building knew he
A fight was determined,[36] since the light of the sun they
No longer could see, and lowering darkness   90
O'er all had descended, and dark under heaven
Shadowy shapes came shying around them.
The liegemen all rose then. One saluted the other,

[*Hrothgar retires, leaving Beowulf in charge of the hall.*]

Hrothgar Beowulf, in rhythmical measures,
Wishing him well, and, the wassail-hall giving
To his care and keeping, quoth he departing:
"Not to any one else have I ever entrusted,
But thee and thee only, the hall of the Danemen,
Since high I could heave my hand and my buckler.
Take thou in charge now the noblest of houses;   100
Be mindful of honor, exhibiting prowess,
Watch 'gainst the foeman! Thou shalt want no enjoyments,
Survive thou safely adventure so glorious!"

XI. All Sleep Save One.

Then Hrothgar departed, his earl-throng attending him,

[*Hrothgar retires.*]

Folk-lord of Scyldings, forth from the building;
The war-chieftain wished then Wealhtheow to look for,
The queen for a bedmate. To keep away Grendel
The Glory of Kings had given a hall-watch,

[*God has provided a watch for the hall.*]

---

[36] Kl. suggests a period after 'determined.' This would give the passage as follows: *Since they no longer could see the light of the sun, and lowering darkness was down over all, dire under the heavens shadowy beings came going around them.*

As men heard recounted: for the king of the Danemen
He did special service, gave the giant a watcher:
And the prince of the Geatmen implicitly trusted
His warlike strength and the Wielder's protection.

[*Beowulf is self-confident.*]

His armor of iron off him he did then,   10

[*He prepares for rest.*]

His helmet from his head, to his henchman committed
His chased-handled chain-sword, choicest of weapons,
And bade him bide with his battle-equipments.
The good one then uttered words of defiance,
Beowulf Geatman, ere his bed he upmounted:
"I hold me no meaner in matters of prowess,

[*Beowulf boasts of his ability to cope with Grendel.*]

In warlike achievements, than Grendel does himself;
Hence I seek not with sword-edge to sooth him to slumber,
Of life to bereave him, though well I am able.
No battle-skill[37] has he, that blows he should strike me,   20

[*We will fight with nature's weapons only.*]

To shatter my shield, though sure he is mighty
In strife and destruction; but struggling by night we
Shall do without edges, dare he to look for
Weaponless warfare, and wise-mooded Father
The glory apportion, God ever-holy,
On which hand soever to him seemeth proper."

[*God may decide who shall conquer.*]

Then the brave-mooded hero bent to his slumber,
The pillow received the cheek of the noble;
And many a martial mere-thane attending

---

[37] Gr. understood 'gódra' as meaning 'advantages in battle.' This rendering H.-So.
rejects. The latter takes the passage as meaning that Grendel, though mighty and
formidable, has no skill in the art of war.

[*The Geatish warriors lie down.*]

Sank to his slumber. Seemed it unlikely   30
That ever thereafter any should hope to

    [*They thought it very unlikely that they should ever see their
       homes again.*]

Be happy at home, hero-friends visit
Or the lordly troop-castle where he lived from his childhood;
They had heard how slaughter had snatched from the wine-hall,
Had recently ravished, of the race of the Scyldings
Too many by far. But the Lord to them granted

    [*But God raised up a deliverer.*]

The weaving of war-speed, to Wederish heroes
Aid and comfort, that every opponent
By one man's war-might they worsted and vanquished,
By the might of himself; the truth is established   40

    [*God rules the world.*]

That God Almighty hath governed for ages
Kindreds and nations. A night very lurid
The trav'ler-at-twilight came tramping and striding.

    [*Grendel comes to Heorot.*]

The warriors were sleeping who should watch the horned-building,
One only excepted. 'Mid earthmen 'twas 'stablished,

    [*Only one warrior is awake.*]

Th' implacable foeman was powerless to hurl them
To the land of shadows, if the Lord were unwilling;
But serving as warder, in terror to foemen,
He angrily bided the issue of battle.[38]

---

[38] B. in his masterly articles on Beowulf (P. and B. XII.) rejects the division usually made at this point, 'Þá.' (711), usually rendered 'then,' he translates 'when,' and connects its clause with the foregoing sentence. These changes he makes to reduce the number of 'cóm's' as principal verbs. (Cf. 703, 711, 721.) With all deference to this acute scholar, I must say that it seems to me that the poet is exhausting his resources to bring out clearly the supreme event on which the whole subsequent action turns. First, he (Grendel) came

XII. Grendel and Beowulf.

'Neath the cloudy cliffs came from the moor then

[*Grendel comes from the fens.*]

Grendel going, God's anger bare he.
The monster intended some one of earthmen
In the hall-building grand to entrap and make way with:
He went under welkin where well he knew of

[*He goes towards the joyous building.*]

The wine-joyous building, brilliant with plating,
Gold-hall of earthmen. Not the earliest occasion
He the home and manor of Hrothgar had sought:

[*This was not his first visit there.*]

Ne'er found he in life-days later nor earlier
Hardier hero, hall-thanes[39] more sturdy!   10
Then came to the building the warrior marching,
Bereft of his joyance. The door quickly opened

[*His horrid fingers tear the door open.*]

On fire-hinges fastened, when his fingers had touched it;
The fell one had flung then—his fury so bitter—
Open the entrance. Early thereafter
The foeman trod the shining hall-pavement,
Strode he angrily; from the eyes of him glimmered

[*He strides furiously into the hall.*]

A lustre unlovely likest to fire.
He beheld in the hall the heroes in numbers,
A circle of kinsmen sleeping together,   20
A throng of thanemen: then his thoughts were exultant,

---

in the wan night; second, he came *from the moor*; third, he came *to the hall.* Time, place from which, place to which, are all given.

[39] B. and t. B. emend so as to make lines 9 and 10 read: N*ever in his life, earlier or later, had he, the hell-thane, found a braver hero.*—They argue that Beowulf's companions had done nothing to merit such encomiums as the usual readings allow them.

[*He exults over his supposed prey.*]

He minded to sunder from each of the thanemen
The life from his body, horrible demon,
Ere morning came, since fate had allowed him
The prospect of plenty. Providence willed not

[*Fate has decreed that he shall devour no more heroes.
Beowulf suffers from suspense.*]

To permit him any more of men under heaven
To eat in the night-time. Higelac's kinsman
Great sorrow endured how the dire-mooded creature
In unlooked-for assaults were likely to bear him.
No thought had the monster of deferring the matter,   30
But on earliest occasion he quickly laid hold of

[*Grendel immediately seizes a sleeping warrior, and devours
him.*]

A soldier asleep, suddenly tore him,
Bit his bone-prison, the blood drank in currents,
Swallowed in mouthfuls: he soon had the dead man's
Feet and hands, too, eaten entirely.
Nearer he strode then, the stout-hearted warrior
Snatched as he slumbered, seizing with hand-grip,

[*Beowulf and Grendel grapple.*]

Forward the foeman foined with his hand;
Caught he quickly the cunning deviser,
On his elbow he rested. This early discovered   40
The master of malice, that in middle-earth's regions,
'Neath the whole of the heavens, no hand-grapple greater
In any man else had he ever encountered:

[*The monster is amazed at Beowulf's strength.*]

Fearful in spirit, faint-mooded waxed he,
Not off could betake him; death he was pondering,
Would fly to his covert, seek the devils' assembly:

[*He is anxious to flee.*]

His calling no more was the same he had followed
Long in his lifetime. The liege-kinsman worthy
Of Higelac minded his speech of the evening,

> [*Beowulf recalls his boast of the evening, and determines to
> fulfil it.*]

Stood he up straight and stoutly did seize him.   50
His fingers crackled; the giant was outward,
The earl stepped farther. The famous one minded
To flee away farther, if he found an occasion,
And off and away, avoiding delay,
To fly to the fen-moors; he fully was ware of
The strength of his grapple in the grip of the foeman.
'Twas an ill-taken journey that the injury-bringing,

> [*'Twas a luckless day for Grendel.*]

Harrying harmer to Heorot wandered:
The palace re-echoed; to all of the Danemen,

> [*The hall groans.*]

Dwellers in castles, to each of the bold ones,   60
Earlmen, was terror. Angry they both were,
Archwarders raging.[40] Rattled the building;
'Twas a marvellous wonder that the wine-hall withstood then
The bold-in-battle, bent not to earthward,
Excellent earth-hall; but within and without it
Was fastened so firmly in fetters of iron,
By the art of the armorer. Off from the sill there
Bent mead-benches many, as men have informed me,
Adorned with gold-work, where the grim ones did struggle.
The Scylding wise men weened ne'er before   70
That by might and main-strength a man under heaven
Might break it in pieces, bone-decked, resplendent,
Crush it by cunning, unless clutch of the fire
In smoke should consume it. The sound mounted upward
Novel enough; on the North Danes fastened

> [*Grendel's cries terrify the Danes.*]

---

[40] For 'réðe rén-weardas' (771), t. B. suggests 'réðe, rénhearde.' Translate: *They
were both angry, raging and mighty.*

A terror of anguish, on all of the men there
Who heard from the wall the weeping and plaining,
The song of defeat from the foeman of heaven,
Heard him hymns of horror howl, and his sorrow
Hell-bound bewailing. He held him too firmly   80
Who was strongest of main-strength of men of that era.

XIII. Grendel Is Vanquished.

For no cause whatever would the earlmen's defender

[*Beowulf has no idea of letting Grendel live.*]

Leave in life-joys the loathsome newcomer,
He deemed his existence utterly useless
To men under heaven. Many a noble
Of Beowulf brandished his battle-sword old,
Would guard the life of his lord and protector,
The far-famous chieftain, if able to do so;
While waging the warfare, this wist they but little,
Brave battle-thanes, while his body intending
To slit into slivers, and seeking his spirit: 10

[*No weapon would harm Grendel; he bore a charmed life.*]

That the relentless foeman nor finest of weapons
Of all on the earth, nor any of war-bills
Was willing to injure; but weapons of victory
Swords and suchlike he had sworn to dispense with.
His death at that time must prove to be wretched,
And the far-away spirit widely should journey
Into enemies' power. This plainly he saw then
Who with mirth[41] of mood malice no little
Had wrought in the past on the race of the earthmen
(To God he was hostile), that his body would fail him,   20
But Higelac's hardy henchman and kinsman
Held him by the hand; hateful to other
Was each one if living. A body-wound suffered

[*Grendel is sorely wounded.*]

---

[41] It has been proposed to translate 'myrðe' by *with sorrow*; but there seems no authority for such a rendering. To the present translator, the phrase 'módes myrðe' seems a mere padding for *gladly*; i.e., *he who gladly harassed mankind.*

The direful demon, damage incurable
Was seen on his shoulder, his sinews were shivered,

[*His body bursts.*]

His body did burst. To Beowulf was given
Glory in battle; Grendel from thenceward
Must flee and hide him in the fen-cliffs and marshes,
Sick unto death, his dwelling must look for
Unwinsome and woful; he wist the more fully   30
The end of his earthly existence was nearing,

[*The monster flees away to hide in the moors.*]

His life-days' limits. At last for the Danemen,
When the slaughter was over, their wish was accomplished.
The comer-from-far-land had cleansed then of evil,
Wise and valiant, the war-hall of Hrothgar,
Saved it from violence. He joyed in the night-work,
In repute for prowess; the prince of the Geatmen
For the East-Danish people his boast had accomplished,
Bettered their burdensome bale-sorrows fully,
The craft-begot evil they erstwhile had suffered   40
And were forced to endure from crushing oppression,
Their manifold misery. 'Twas a manifest token,
When the hero-in-battle the hand suspended,
The arm and the shoulder (there was all of the claw

[*Beowulf suspends Grendel's hand and arm in Heorot.*]

Of Grendel together) 'neath great-stretching hall-roof.

XIV. Rejoicing of the Danes.

In the mist of the morning many a warrior

[*At early dawn, warriors from far and near come together to
    hear of the night's adventures.*]

Stood round the gift-hall, as the story is told me:
Folk-princes fared then from far and from near
Through long-stretching journeys to look at the wonder,
The footprints of the foeman. Few of the warriors
Who gazed on the foot-tracks of the inglorious creature

[Few warriors lamented Grendel's destruction.]

His parting from life pained very deeply,
How, weary in spirit, off from those regions
In combats conquered he carried his traces,
Fated and flying, to the flood of the nickers.   10
There in bloody billows bubbled the currents,

[Grendel's blood dyes the waters.]

The angry eddy was everywhere mingled
And seething with gore, welling with sword-blood;[42]
He death-doomed had hid him, when reaved of his joyance
He laid down his life in the lair he had fled to,
His heathenish spirit, where hell did receive him.
Thence the friends from of old backward turned them,
And many a younker from merry adventure,
Striding their stallions, stout from the seaward,
Heroes on horses. There were heard very often   20
Beowulf's praises; many often asserted

[Beowulf is the hero of the hour.]

That neither south nor north, in the circuit of waters,
O'er outstretching earth-plain, none other was better

[He is regarded as a probable successor to Hrothgar.]

'Mid bearers of war-shields, more worthy to govern,
'Neath the arch of the ether. Not any, however,
'Gainst the friend-lord muttered, mocking-words uttered
Of Hrothgar the gracious (a good king he).

[But no word is uttered to derogate from the old king.]

Oft the famed ones permitted their fallow-skinned horses
To run in rivalry, racing and chasing,
Where the fieldways appeared to them fair and inviting,   30
Known for their excellence; oft a thane of the folk-lord,[43]

---

[42] S. emends, suggesting 'déop' for 'déog,' and removing semicolon after 'wéol.'
The two half-lines 'welling ... hid him' would then read: *The bloody deep welled with sword-gore.* B. accepts 'déop' for 'déog,' but reads 'déað-fæges': *The deep boiled with the sword-gore of the death-doomed one.*

[44]A man of celebrity, mindful of rhythms,

[*The gleeman sings the deeds of heroes.*]

Who ancient traditions treasured in memory,
New word-groups found properly bound:
The bard after 'gan then Beowulf's venture
Wisely to tell of, and words that were clever

[*He sings in alliterative measures of Beowulf's prowess.*]

To utter skilfully, earnestly speaking,
Everything told he that he heard as to Sigmund's
Mighty achievements, many things hidden,

[*Also of Sigemund, who has slain a great fire-dragon.*]

The strife of the Wælsing, the wide-going ventures   40
The children of men knew of but little,
The feud and the fury, but Fitela with him,
When suchlike matters he minded to speak of,
Uncle to nephew, as in every contention
Each to other was ever devoted:
A numerous host of the race of the scathers
They had slain with the sword-edge. To Sigmund accrued then
No little of glory, when his life-days were over,
Since he sturdy in struggle had destroyed the great dragon,
The hoard-treasure's keeper; 'neath the hoar-grayish stone he,   50
The son of the atheling, unaided adventured
The perilous project; not present was Fitela,
Yet the fortune befell him of forcing his weapon
Through the marvellous dragon, that it stood in the wall,
Well-honored weapon; the worm was slaughtered.
The great one had gained then by his glorious achievement
To reap from the ring-hoard richest enjoyment,
As best it did please him: his vessel he loaded,
Shining ornaments on the ship's bosom carried,
Kinsman of Wæls: the drake in heat melted.   60
He was farthest famed of fugitive pilgrims,

---

[43] Another and quite different rendering of this passage is as follows: *Oft a liegeman of the king, a fame-covered man mindful of songs, who very many ancient traditions remembered (he found other word-groups accurately bound together) began afterward to tell of Beowulf's adventure, skilfully to narrate it, etc.*

[44] Might 'guma gilp-hladen' mean 'a man laden with boasts of the deeds of others'?

[*Sigemund was widely famed.*]

Mid wide-scattered world-folk, for works of great prowess,
War-troopers' shelter: hence waxed he in honor.[45]
Afterward Heremod's hero-strength failed him,

[*Heremod, an unfortunate Danish king, is introduced by way
of contrast.*]

His vigor and valor. 'Mid venomous haters
To the hands of foemen he was foully delivered,
Offdriven early. Agony-billows
Oppressed him too long, to his people he became then,

[*Unlike Sigemund and Beowulf, Heremod was a burden to his
people.*]

To all the athelings, an ever-great burden;
And the daring one's journey in days of yore   70
Many wise men were wont to deplore,
Such as hoped he would bring them help in their sorrow,
That the son of their ruler should rise into power,
Holding the headship held by his fathers,
Should govern the people, the gold-hoard and borough,
The kingdom of heroes, the realm of the Scyldings.
He to all men became then far more beloved,

[*Beowulf is an honor to his race.*]

Higelac's kinsman, to kindreds and races,
To his friends much dearer; him malice assaulted.—
Oft running and racing on roadsters they measured   80

[*The story is resumed.*]

The dun-colored highways. Then the light of the morning
Was hurried and hastened. Went henchmen in numbers
To the beautiful building, bold ones in spirit,
To look at the wonder; the liegelord himself then
From his wife-bower wending, warden of treasures,
Glorious trod with troopers unnumbered,

---

[45] t. B. accepts B.'s 'hé þæs áron þáh' as given by H.-So., but puts a comma after
'þáh,' and takes 'siððan' as introducing a dependent clause: *He throve in honor since
Heremod's strength ... had decreased.*

Famed for his virtues, and with him the queen-wife
Measured the mead-ways, with maidens attending.

XV. Hrothgar's Gratitude.

Hrothgar discoursed (to the hall-building went he,
He stood by the pillar,[46] saw the steep-rising hall-roof
Gleaming with gold-gems, and Grendel his hand there):
"For the sight we behold now, thanks to the Wielder

[*Hrothgar gives thanks for the overthrow of the monster.*]

Early be offered! Much evil I bided,
Snaring from Grendel:[47] God can e'er 'complish
Wonder on wonder, Wielder of Glory!
But lately I reckoned ne'er under heaven

[*I had given up all hope, when this brave liegeman came to our aid.*]

Comfort to gain me for any of sorrows,
While the handsomest of houses horrid with bloodstain   10
Gory uptowered; grief had offfrightened[48]
Each of the wise ones who weened not that ever
The folk-troop's defences 'gainst foes they should strengthen,
'Gainst sprites and monsters. Through the might of the Wielder
A doughty retainer hath a deed now accomplished
Which erstwhile we all with our excellent wisdom
Failed to perform. May affirm very truly

[*If his mother yet liveth, well may she thank God for this son.*]

What woman soever in all of the nations
Gave birth to the child, if yet she surviveth,
That the long-ruling Lord was lavish to herward   20
In the birth of the bairn. Now, Beowulf dear,
Most excellent hero, I'll love thee in spirit

[*Hereafter, Beowulf, thou shalt be my son.*]

---

[46] B. and t. B. read 'staþole,' and translate *stood on the floor.*

[47] For 'snaring from Grendel,' 'sorrows at Grendel's hands' has been suggested. This gives a parallel to 'láðes.' 'Grynna' may well be gen. pl. of 'gyrn,' by a scribal slip.

[48] The H.-So punctuation has been followed; but B. has been followed in understanding 'gehwylcne' as object of 'wíd-scofen (hæfde).' Gr. construes 'wéa' as nom abs.

As bairn of my body; bear well henceforward
The relationship new. No lack shall befall thee
Of earth-joys any I ever can give thee.
Full often for lesser service I've given
Hero less hardy hoard-treasure precious,
To a weaker in war-strife. By works of distinction

[*Thou hast won immortal distinction.*]

Thou hast gained for thyself now that thy glory shall flourish
Forever and ever. The All-Ruler quite thee   30
With good from His hand as He hitherto did thee!"
Beowulf answered, Ecgtheow's offspring:

[*Beowulf replies: I was most happy to render thee this
service.*]

"That labor of glory most gladly achieved we,
The combat accomplished, unquailing we ventured
The enemy's grapple; I would grant it much rather
Thou wert able to look at the creature in person,
Faint unto falling, the foe in his trappings!
On murder-bed quickly I minded to bind him,
With firm-holding fetters, that forced by my grapple
Low he should lie in life-and-death struggle   40
'Less his body escape; I was wholly unable,
Since God did not will it, to keep him from going,

[*I could not keep the monster from escaping, as God did not
will that I should.*]

Not held him that firmly, hated opposer;
Too swift was the foeman. Yet safety regarding
He suffered his hand behind him to linger,
His arm and shoulder, to act as watcher;
No shadow of solace the woe-begone creature

[*He left his hand and arm behind.*]

Found him there nathless: the hated destroyer
Liveth no longer, lashed for his evils,
But sorrow hath seized him, in snare-meshes hath him   50
Close in its clutches, keepeth him writhing
In baleful bonds: there banished for evil
The man shall wait for the mighty tribunal,

How the God of glory shall give him his earnings."

[God will give him his deserts.]

Then the soldier kept silent, son of old Ecglaf,
From boasting and bragging of battle-achievements,

*[Unferth has nothing more to say, for Beowulf's actions speak
    louder than words.]*

Since the princes beheld there the hand that depended
'Neath the lofty hall-timbers by the might of the nobleman,
Each one before him, the enemy's fingers;
Each finger-nail strong steel most resembled,   60
The heathen one's hand-spur, the hero-in-battle's
Claw most uncanny; quoth they agreeing,
That not any excellent edges of brave ones

[No sword will harm the monster.]

Was willing to touch him, the terrible creature's
Battle-hand bloody to bear away from him.

    XVI. Hrothgar Lavishes Gifts Upon His Deliverer.

Then straight was ordered that Heorot inside[49]

[Heorot is adorned with hands.]

With hands be embellished: a host of them gathered,
Of men and women, who the wassailing-building
The guest-hall begeared. Gold-flashing sparkled
Webs on the walls then, of wonders a many
To each of the heroes that look on such objects.
The beautiful building was broken to pieces

[The hall is defaced, however.]

---

[49] Kl. suggests 'hroden' for 'háten,' and renders: *Then quickly was Heorot adorned
within, with hands bedecked.*—B. suggests 'gefrætwon' instead of 'gefrætwod,' and
renders: *Then was it commanded to adorn Heorot within quickly with hands.*—The
former has the advantage of affording a parallel to 'gefrætwod': both have the
disadvantage of altering the text.

Which all within with irons was fastened,
Its hinges torn off: only the roof was
Whole and uninjured when the horrible creature 10
Outlawed for evil off had betaken him,
Hopeless of living. 'Tis hard to avoid it
(Whoever will do it!); but he doubtless must come to[50]

[*A vague passage of five verses.*]

The place awaiting, as Wyrd hath appointed,
Soul-bearers, earth-dwellers, earls under heaven,
Where bound on its bed his body shall slumber
When feasting is finished. Full was the time then

[*Hrothgar goes to the banquet.*]

That the son of Healfdene went to the building;
The excellent atheling would eat of the banquet.
Ne'er heard I that people with hero-band larger 20
Bare them better tow'rds their bracelet-bestower.
The laden-with-glory stooped to the bench then
(Their kinsmen-companions in plenty were joyful,
Many a cupful quaffing complaisantly),
Doughty of spirit in the high-tow'ring palace,
Hrothgar and Hrothulf. Heorot then inside

[*Hrothgar's nephew, Hrothulf, is present.*]

Was filled with friendly ones; falsehood and treachery
The Folk-Scyldings now nowise did practise.
Then the offspring of Healfdene offered to Beowulf

[*Hrothgar lavishes gifts upon Beowulf.*]

A golden standard, as reward for the victory, 30
A banner embossed, burnie and helmet;
Many men saw then a song-famous weapon
Borne 'fore the hero. Beowulf drank of
The cup in the building; that treasure-bestowing

---

[50] The passage 1005-1009 seems to be hopeless. One difficult point is to find a subject for 'gesacan.' Some say 'he'; others supply 'each,' *i.e., every soul-bearer ... must gain the inevitable place.* The genitives in this case are partitive.—If 'he' be subj., the genitives are dependent on 'gearwe' (= prepared).—The 'he' itself is disputed, some referring it to Grendel; but B. takes it as involved in the parenthesis.

He needed not blush for in battle-men's presence.

[*Four handsomer gifts were never presented.*]

Ne'er heard I that many men on the ale-bench
In friendlier fashion to their fellows presented
Four bright jewels with gold-work embellished.
'Round the roof of the helmet a head-guarder outside
Braided with wires, with bosses was furnished,   40
That swords-for-the-battle fight-hardened might fail
Boldly to harm him, when the hero proceeded
Forth against foemen. The defender of earls then

[*Hrothgar commands that eight finely caparisoned steeds be
brought to Beowulf.*]

Commanded that eight steeds with bridles
Gold-plated, gleaming, be guided to hallward,
Inside the building; on one of them stood then
An art-broidered saddle embellished with jewels;
'Twas the sovereign's seat, when the son of King Healfdene
Was pleased to take part in the play of the edges;
The famous one's valor ne'er failed at the front when   50
Slain ones were bowing. And to Beowulf granted
The prince of the Ingwins, power over both,
O'er war-steeds and weapons; bade him well to enjoy them.
In so manly a manner the mighty-famed chieftain,
Hoard-ward of heroes, with horses and jewels
War-storms requited, that none e'er condemneth
Who willeth to tell truth with full justice.

XVII. Banquet (continued).—The Scop's Song of Finn and Hnæf.

And the atheling of earlmen to each of the heroes

[*Each of Beowulf's companions receives a costly gift.*]

Who the ways of the waters went with Beowulf,
A costly gift-token gave on the mead-bench,
Offered an heirloom, and ordered that that man
With gold should be paid for, whom Grendel had erstwhile

[*The warrior killed by Grendel is to be paid for in gold.*]

Wickedly slaughtered, as he more of them had done
Had far-seeing God and the mood of the hero
The fate not averted: the Father then governed
All of the earth-dwellers, as He ever is doing;
Hence insight for all men is everywhere fittest,   10
Forethought of spirit! much he shall suffer
Of lief and of loathsome who long in this present
Useth the world in this woful existence.
There was music and merriment mingling together
Touching Healfdene's leader; the joy-wood was fingered,

> [*Hrothgar's scop recalls events in the reign of his lord's
> father.*]

Measures recited, when the singer of Hrothgar
On mead-bench should mention the merry hall-joyance
Of the kinsmen of Finn, when onset surprised them:
"The Half-Danish hero, Hnæf of the Scyldings,

> [*Hnæf, the Danish general, is treacherously attacked while
> staying at Finn's castle.*]

On the field of the Frisians was fated to perish.   20
Sure Hildeburg needed not mention approving
The faith of the Jutemen: though blameless entirely,
When shields were shivered she was shorn of her darlings,

> [*Queen Hildeburg is not only wife of Finn, but a kinswoman of
> the murdered Hnæf.*]

Of bairns and brothers: they bent to their fate
With war-spear wounded; woe was that woman.
Not causeless lamented the daughter of Hoce
The decree of the Wielder when morning-light came and
She was able 'neath heaven to behold the destruction
Of brothers and bairns, where the brightest of earth-joys
She had hitherto had: all the henchmen of Finn   30

> [*Finn's force is almost exterminated.*]

War had offtaken, save a handful remaining,
That he nowise was able to offer resistance[51]
To the onset of Hengest in the parley of battle,

[*Hengest succeeds Hnæf as Danish general.*]

Nor the wretched remnant to rescue in war from
The earl of the atheling; but they offered conditions,
Another great building to fully make ready,

[*Compact between the Frisians and the Danes.*]

A hall and a high-seat, that half they might rule with
The sons of the Jutemen, and that Folcwalda's son would
Day after day the Danemen honor
When gifts were giving, and grant of his ring-store   40
To Hengest's earl-troop ever so freely,
Of his gold-plated jewels, as he encouraged the Frisians
On the bench of the beer-hall. On both sides they swore then

[*Equality of gifts agreed on.*]

A fast-binding compact; Finn unto Hengest
With no thought of revoking vowed then most solemnly
The woe-begone remnant well to take charge of,
His Witan advising; the agreement should no one
By words or works weaken and shatter,
By artifice ever injure its value,
Though reaved of their ruler their ring-giver's slayer   50
They followed as vassals, Fate so requiring:
Then if one of the Frisians the quarrel should speak of

[*No one shall refer to old grudges.*]

In tones that were taunting, terrible edges
Should cut in requital. Accomplished the oath was,
And treasure of gold from the hoard was uplifted.
The best of the Scylding braves was then fully

[*Danish warriors are burned on a funeral-pyre.*]

---

[51] For 1084, R. suggests 'wiht Hengeste wið gefeohtan.'—K. suggests 'wið Hengeste wiht gefeohtan.' Neither emendation would make any essential change in the translation.

Prepared for the pile; at the pyre was seen clearly
The blood-gory burnie, the boar with his gilding,
The iron-hard swine, athelings many
Fatally wounded; no few had been slaughtered. 60
Hildeburg bade then, at the burning of Hnæf,
The bairn of her bosom to bear to the fire,

[*Queen Hildeburg has her son burnt along with Hnæf.*]

That his body be burned and borne to the pyre.
The woe-stricken woman wept on his shoulder,[52]
In measures lamented; upmounted the hero.[53]
The greatest of dead-fires curled to the welkin,
On the hill's-front crackled; heads were a-melting,
Wound-doors bursting, while the blood was a-coursing
From body-bite fierce. The fire devoured them,
Greediest of spirits, whom war had offcarried 70
From both of the peoples; their bravest were fallen.

XVIII. The Finn Episode (continued).—The Banquet Continues.

"Then the warriors departed to go to their dwellings,

[*The survivors go to Friesland, the home of Finn.*]

Reaved of their friends, Friesland to visit,
Their homes and high-city. Hengest continued
Biding with Finn the blood-tainted winter,

[*Hengest remains there all winter, unable to get away.*]

---

[52] The separation of adjective and noun by a phrase (cf. v. 1118) being very unusual, some scholars have put 'earme on eaxle' with the foregoing lines, inserting a semicolon after 'eaxle.' In this case 'on eaxe' (i.e., on the ashes, cinders) is sometimes read, and this affords a parallel to 'on bæl.' Let us hope that a satisfactory rendering shall yet be reached without resorting to any tampering with the text, such as Lichtenheld proposed: 'earme ides on eaxle gnornode.'

[53] For 'gúð-rinc,' 'gúð-réc,' *battle-smoke*, has been suggested.

Wholly unsundered;[54] of fatherland thought he
Though unable to drive the ring-stemmèd vessel
O'er the ways of the waters; the wave-deeps were tossing,
Fought with the wind; winter in ice-bonds
Closed up the currents, till there came to the dwelling
A year in its course, as yet it revolveth,   10
If season propitious one alway regardeth,
World-cheering weathers. Then winter was gone,
Earth's bosom was lovely; the exile would get him,
The guest from the palace; on grewsomest vengeance

[*He devises schemes of vengeance.*]

He brooded more eager than on oversea journeys,
Whe'r onset-of-anger he were able to 'complish,
The bairns of the Jutemen therein to remember.
Nowise refused he the duties of liegeman
When Hun of the Frisians the battle-sword Láfing,
Fairest of falchions, friendly did give him: 20
Its edges were famous in folk-talk of Jutland.
And savage sword-fury seized in its clutches
Bold-mooded Finn where he bode in his palace,
When the grewsome grapple Guthlaf and Oslaf

[*Guthlaf and Oslaf revenge Hnæf's slaughter.*]

Had mournfully mentioned, the mere-journey over,
For sorrows half-blamed him; the flickering spirit
Could not bide in his bosom. Then the building was covered[55]
With corpses of foemen, and Finn too was slaughtered,

[*Finn is slain.*]

---

[54] For 1130 (1) R. and Gr. suggest 'elne unflitme' as 1098 (1) reads. The latter verse is undisputed; and, for the former, 'elne' would be as possible as 'ealles,' and 'unflitme' is well supported. Accepting 'elne unflitme' for both, I would suggest '*very peaceably*' for both places: (1) *Finn to Hengest very peaceably vowed with oaths, etc.* (2) *Hengest then still the slaughter-stained winter remained there with Finn very peaceably.* The two passages become thus correlatives, the second a sequel of the first. 'Elne,' in the sense of very (swíðe), needs no argument; and 'unflitme' (from 'flítan') can, it seems to me, be more plausibly rendered 'peaceful,' 'peaceable,' than 'contestable,' or 'conquerable.'

[55] Some scholars have proposed 'roden'; the line would then read: *Then the building was reddened, etc.*, instead of 'covered.' The 'h' may have been carried over from the three alliterating 'h's.'

The king with his comrades, and the queen made a prisoner.
The troops of the Scyldings bore to their vessels   30

[*The jewels of Finn, and his queen are carried away by the
Danes.*]

All that the land-king had in his palace,
Such trinkets and treasures they took as, on searching,
At Finn's they could find. They ferried to Daneland
The excellent woman on oversea journey,
Led her to their land-folk." The lay was concluded,

[*The lay is concluded, and the main story is resumed.*]

The gleeman's recital. Shouts again rose then,
Bench-glee resounded, bearers then offered
Wine from wonder-vats. Wealhtheo advanced then

[*Skinkers carry round the beaker.*]

Going 'neath gold-crown, where the good ones were seated
Uncle and nephew; their peace was yet mutual,   40

[*Queen Wealhtheow greets Hrothgar, as he sits beside
Hrothulf, his nephew.*]

True each to the other. And Unferth the spokesman
Sat at the feet of the lord of the Scyldings:
Each trusted his spirit that his mood was courageous,
Though at fight he had failed in faith to his kinsmen.
Said the queen of the Scyldings: "My lord and protector,
Treasure-bestower, take thou this beaker;
Joyance attend thee, gold-friend of heroes,
And greet thou the Geatmen with gracious responses!

[*Be generous to the Geats.*]

So ought one to do. Be kind to the Geatmen,
In gifts not niggardly; anear and afar now   50
Peace thou enjoyest. Report hath informed me
Thou'lt have for a bairn the battle-brave hero.
Now is Heorot cleansèd, ring-palace gleaming;
Give while thou mayest many rewards,

[Have as much joy as possible in thy hall, once more purified.]

And bequeath to thy kinsmen kingdom and people,
On wending thy way to the Wielder's splendor.
I know good Hrothulf, that the noble young troopers
He'll care for and honor, lord of the Scyldings,

[I know that Hrothulf will prove faithful if he survive thee.]

If earth-joys thou endest earlier than he doth;
I reckon that recompense he'll render with kindness   60
Our offspring and issue, if that all he remember,
What favors of yore, when he yet was an infant,
We awarded to him for his worship and pleasure."
Then she turned by the bench where her sons were carousing,
Hrethric and Hrothmund, and the heroes' offspring,
The war-youth together; there the good one was sitting

[Beowulf is sitting by the two royal sons.]

'Twixt the brothers twain, Beowulf Geatman.

XIX. Beowulf Receives Further Honor.

A beaker was borne him, and bidding to quaff it

[More gifts are offered Beowulf.]

Graciously given, and gold that was twisted
Pleasantly proffered, a pair of arm-jewels,
Rings and corslet, of collars the greatest
I've heard of 'neath heaven. Of heroes not any
More splendid from jewels have I heard 'neath the welkin,
Since Hama off bore the Brosingmen's necklace,

[A famous necklace is referred to, in comparison with the gems presented to Beowulf.]

The bracteates and jewels, from the bright-shining city,[56]
Eormenric's cunning craftiness fled from,
Chose gain everlasting. Geatish Higelac,   10
Grandson of Swerting, last had this jewel
When tramping 'neath banner the treasure he guarded,

---

[56] C. suggests a semicolon after 'city,' with 'he' as supplied subject of 'fled' and 'chose.'

The field-spoil defended; Fate offcarried him
When for deeds of daring he endured tribulation,
Hate from the Frisians; the ornaments bare he
O'er the cup of the currents, costly gem-treasures,
Mighty folk-leader, he fell 'neath his target;
The[57] corpse of the king then came into charge of
The race of the Frankmen, the mail-shirt and collar:
Warmen less noble plundered the fallen,   20
When the fight was finished; the folk of the Geatmen
The field of the dead held in possession.
The choicest of mead-halls with cheering resounded.
Wealhtheo discoursed, the war-troop addressed she:
"This collar enjoy thou, Beowulf worthy,

[*Queen Wealhtheow magnifies Beowulf's achievements.*]

Young man, in safety, and use thou this armor,
Gems of the people, and prosper thou fully,
Show thyself sturdy and be to these liegemen
Mild with instruction! I'll mind thy requital.
Thou hast brought it to pass that far and near   30
Forever and ever earthmen shall honor thee,
Even so widely as ocean surroundeth
The blustering bluffs. Be, while thou livest,
A wealth-blessèd atheling. I wish thee most truly
Jewels and treasure. Be kind to my son, thou

[*May gifts never fail thee.*]

Living in joyance! Here each of the nobles
Is true unto other, gentle in spirit,
Loyal to leader. The liegemen are peaceful,
The war-troops ready: well-drunken heroes,[58]
Do as I bid ye." Then she went to the settle.   40
There was choicest of banquets, wine drank the heroes:
Weird they knew not, destiny cruel,

[*They little know of the sorrow in store for them.*]

---

[57] For 'feorh' S. suggests 'feoh': 'corpse' in the translation would then be changed to '*possessions*,' '*belongings.*' This is a better reading than one joining, in such intimate syntactical relations, things so unlike as 'corpse' and 'jewels.'

[58] S. suggests '*wine-joyous heroes*,' '*warriors elated with wine.*'

As to many an earlman early it happened,
When evening had come and Hrothgar had parted
Off to his manor, the mighty to slumber.
Warriors unnumbered warded the building
As erst they did often: the ale-settle bared they,
'Twas covered all over with beds and pillows.
Doomed unto death, down to his slumber

[*A doomed thane is there with them.*]

Bowed then a beer-thane. Their battle-shields placed they,   50
Bright-shining targets, up by their heads then;
O'er the atheling on ale-bench 'twas easy to see there
Battle-high helmet, burnie of ring-mail,
And mighty war-spear. 'Twas the wont of that people

[*They were always ready for battle.*]

To constantly keep them equipped for the battle,[59]
At home or marching—in either condition—
At seasons just such as necessity ordered
As best for their ruler; that people was worthy.

XX. The Mother of Grendel.

They sank then to slumber. With sorrow one paid for
His evening repose, as often betid them
While Grendel was holding[60] the gold-bedecked palace,
Ill-deeds performing, till his end overtook him,
Death for his sins. 'Twas seen very clearly,
Known unto earth-folk, that still an avenger

[*Grendel's mother is known to be thirsting for revenge.*]

---

[59] I believe this translation brings out the meaning of the poet, without departing seriously from the H.-So. text. 'Oft' frequently means 'constantly,' 'continually,' not always 'often.'—Why 'an (on) wíg gearwe' should be written 'ánwíg-gearwe' (= ready for single combat), I cannot see. 'Gearwe' occurs quite frequently with 'on'; cf. B. 1110 (*ready for the pyre*), El. 222 (*ready for the glad journey*). Moreover, what has the idea of single combat to do with B. 1247 ff.? The poet is giving an inventory of the arms and armor which they lay aside on retiring, and he closes his narration by saying that they were *always prepared for battle both at home and on the march.*

[60] Several eminent authorities either read or emend the MS. so as to make this verse read, *While Grendel was wasting the gold-bedecked palace.* So 20 15 below: *ravaged the desert.*

Outlived the loathed one, long since the sorrow
Caused by the struggle; the mother of Grendel,
Devil-shaped woman, her woe ever minded,
Who was held to inhabit the horrible waters,   10
The cold-flowing currents, after Cain had become a

[*Grendel's progenitor, Cain, is again referred to.*]

Slayer-with-edges to his one only brother,
The son of his sire; he set out then banished,
Marked as a murderer, man-joys avoiding,
Lived in the desert. Thence demons unnumbered
Fate-sent awoke; one of them Grendel,

[*The poet again magnifies Beowulf's valor.*]

Sword-cursèd, hateful, who at Heorot met with
A man that was watching, waiting the struggle,
Where a horrid one held him with hand-grapple sturdy;
Nathless he minded the might of his body,   20
The glorious gift God had allowed him,
And folk-ruling Father's favor relied on,
His help and His comfort: so he conquered the foeman,
The hell-spirit humbled: he unhappy departed then,
Reaved of his joyance, journeying to death-haunts,
Foeman of man. His mother moreover
Eager and gloomy was anxious to go on

[*Grendel's mother comes to avenge her son.*]

Her mournful mission, mindful of vengeance
For the death of her son. She came then to Heorot
Where the Armor-Dane earlmen all through the building   30
Were lying in slumber. Soon there became then
Return[61] to the nobles, when the mother of Grendel
Entered the folk-hall; the fear was less grievous
By even so much as the vigor of maidens,
War-strength of women, by warrior is reckoned,
When well-carved weapon, worked with the hammer,
Blade very bloody, brave with its edges,
Strikes down the boar-sign that stands on the helmet.
Then the hard-edgèd weapon was heaved in the building,[62]

---

[61] For 'sóna' (1281), t. B. suggests 'sára,' limiting 'edhwyrft.' Read then: *Return of sorrows to the nobles, etc.* This emendation supplies the syntactical gap after 'edhwyrft.'

The brand o'er the benches, broad-lindens many   40
Hand-fast were lifted; for helmet he recked not,
For armor-net broad, whom terror laid hold of.
She went then hastily, outward would get her
Her life for to save, when some one did spy her;
Soon she had grappled one of the athelings

[She seizes a favorite liegemen of Hrothgar's.]

Fast and firmly, when fenward she hied her;
That one to Hrothgar was liefest of heroes
In rank of retainer where waters encircle,
A mighty shield-warrior, whom she murdered at slumber,
A broadly-famed battle-knight. Beowulf was absent,   50
But another apartment was erstwhile devoted

[Beowulf was asleep in another part of the palace.]

To the glory-decked Geatman when gold was distributed.
There was hubbub in Heorot. The hand that was famous
She grasped in its gore;[63] grief was renewed then
In homes and houses: 'twas no happy arrangement
In both of the quarters to barter and purchase
With lives of their friends. Then the well-agèd ruler,
The gray-headed war-thane, was woful in spirit,
When his long-trusted liegeman lifeless he knew of,
His dearest one gone. Quick from a room was   60

[Beowulf is sent for.]

Beowulf brought, brave and triumphant.
As day was dawning in the dusk of the morning,
Went then that earlman, champion noble,

[He comes at Hrothgar's summons.]

---

[62] Some authorities follow Grein's lexicon in treating 'heard ecg' as an adj. limiting 'sweord': H.-So. renders it as a subst. (So v. 1491.) The sense of the translation would be the same.
[63] B. suggests 'under hróf genam' (v. 1303). This emendation, as well as an emendation with (?) to v. 739, he offers, because 'under' baffles him in both passages. All we need is to take 'under' in its secondary meaning of 'in,' which, though not given by Grein, occurs in the literature. Cf. Chron. 876 (March's A.-S. Gram. § 355) and Oro. Amaz. I. 10, where 'under' = *in the midst of.* Cf. modern Eng. 'in such circumstances,' which interchanges in good usage with 'under such circumstances.'

Came with comrades, where the clever one bided
Whether God all gracious would grant him a respite
After the woe he had suffered. The war-worthy hero
With a troop of retainers trod then the pavement
(The hall-building groaned), till he greeted the wise one,
The earl of the Ingwins;[64] asked if the night had

[*Beowulf inquires how Hrothgar had enjoyed his night's rest.*]

Fully refreshed him, as fain he would have it.   70

XXI. Hrothgar's Account of the Monsters.

Hrothgar rejoined, helm of the Scyldings:

[*Hrothgar laments the death of Æschere, his shoulder-companion.*]

"Ask not of joyance! Grief is renewed to
The folk of the Danemen. Dead is Æschere,
Yrmenlaf's brother, older than he,
My true-hearted counsellor, trusty adviser,
Shoulder-companion, when fighting in battle
Our heads we protected, when troopers were clashing,
And heroes were dashing; such an earl should be ever,

[*He was my ideal hero.*]

An erst-worthy atheling, as Æschere proved him.
The flickering death-spirit became in Heorot   10
His hand-to-hand murderer; I can not tell whither
The cruel one turned in the carcass exulting,
By cramming discovered.[65] The quarrel she wreaked then,

[*This horrible creature came to avenge Grendel's death.*]

That last night igone Grendel thou killedst
In grewsomest manner, with grim-holding clutches,
Since too long he had lessened my liege-troop and wasted
My folk-men so foully. He fell in the battle

---

[64] For 'néod-laðu' (1321) C. suggests 'néad-láðum,' and translates: *asked whether the night had been pleasant to him after crushing-hostility.*

[65] For 'gefrægnod' (1334), K. and t. B. suggest 'gefægnod,' rendering '*rejoicing in her fill.*' This gives a parallel to 'æse wlanc' (1333).

With forfeit of life, and another has followed,
A mighty crime-worker, her kinsman avenging,
And henceforth hath 'stablished her hatred unyielding,[66]   20
As it well may appear to many a liegeman,
Who mourneth in spirit the treasure-bestower,
Her heavy heart-sorrow; the hand is now lifeless
Which[67] availed you in every wish that you cherished.
Land-people heard I, liegemen, this saying,

> *[I have heard my vassals speak of these two uncanny monsters
> who lived in the moors.]*

Dwellers in halls, they had seen very often
A pair of such mighty march-striding creatures,
Far-dwelling spirits, holding the moorlands:
One of them wore, as well they might notice,
The image of woman, the other one wretched   30
In guise of a man wandered in exile,
Except he was huger than any of earthmen;
Earth-dwelling people entitled him Grendel
In days of yore: they know not their father,
Whe'r ill-going spirits any were borne him
Ever before. They guard the wolf-coverts,

> *[The inhabit the most desolate and horrible places.]*

Lands inaccessible, wind-beaten nesses,
Fearfullest fen-deeps, where a flood from the mountains
'Neath mists of the nesses netherward rattles,
The stream under earth: not far is it henceward   40
Measured by mile-lengths that the mere-water standeth,
Which forests hang over, with frost-whiting covered,[68]
A firm-rooted forest, the floods overshadow.
There ever at night one an ill-meaning portent
A fire-flood may see; 'mong children of men
None liveth so wise that wot of the bottom;
Though harassed by hounds the heath-stepper seek for,
Fly to the forest, firm-antlered he-deer,

---

[66] The line 'And ... yielding,' B. renders: *And she has performed a deed of blood-vengeance whose effect is far-reaching.*

[67] 'Sé Þe' (1345) is an instance of masc. rel. with fem. antecedent. So v. 1888, where 'sé Þe' refers to 'yldo.'

[68] For 'hrímge' in the H.-So. edition, Gr. and others read 'hrínde' (=hrínende), and translate: *which rustling forests overhang.*

[*Even the hounded deer will not seek refuge in these uncanny regions.*]

Spurred from afar, his spirit he yieldeth,
His life on the shore, ere in he will venture   50
To cover his head. Uncanny the place is:
Thence upward ascendeth the surging of waters,
Wan to the welkin, when the wind is stirring
The weathers unpleasing, till the air groweth gloomy,
And the heavens lower. Now is help to be gotten

[*To thee only can I look for assistance.*]

From thee and thee only! The abode thou know'st not,
The dangerous place where thou'rt able to meet with
The sin-laden hero: seek if thou darest!
For the feud I will fully fee thee with money,
With old-time treasure, as erstwhile I did thee,   60
With well-twisted jewels, if away thou shalt get thee."

XXII. Beowulf Seeks Grendel's Mother.

Beowulf answered, Ecgtheow's son:
"Grieve not, O wise one! for each it is better,

[*Beowulf exhorts the old king to arouse himself for action.*]

His friend to avenge than with vehemence wail him;
Each of us must the end-day abide of
His earthly existence; who is able accomplish
Glory ere death! To battle-thane noble
Lifeless lying, 'tis at last most fitting.
Arise, O king, quick let us hasten
To look at the footprint of the kinsman of Grendel!
I promise thee this now: to his place he'll escape not,   10
To embrace of the earth, nor to mountainous forest,
Nor to depths of the ocean, wherever he wanders.
Practice thou now patient endurance
Of each of thy sorrows, as I hope for thee soothly!"
Then up sprang the old one, the All-Wielder thanked he,

[*Hrothgar rouses himself. His horse is brought.*]

Ruler Almighty, that the man had outspoken.
Then for Hrothgar a war-horse was decked with a bridle,
Curly-maned courser. The clever folk-leader
Stately proceeded: stepped then an earl-troop

[*They start on the track of the female monster.*]

Of linden-wood bearers. Her footprints were seen then   20
Widely in wood-paths, her way o'er the bottoms,
Where she faraway fared o'er fen-country murky,
Bore away breathless the best of retainers
Who pondered with Hrothgar the welfare of country.
The son of the athelings then went o'er the stony,
Declivitous cliffs, the close-covered passes,
Narrow passages, paths unfrequented,
Nesses abrupt, nicker-haunts many;
One of a few of wise-mooded heroes,
He onward advanced to view the surroundings,   30
Till he found unawares woods of the mountain
O'er hoar-stones hanging, holt-wood unjoyful;
The water stood under, welling and gory.
'Twas irksome in spirit to all of the Danemen,
Friends of the Scyldings, to many a liegeman
Sad to be suffered, a sorrow unlittle

[*The sight of Æschere's head causes them great sorrow.*]

To each of the earlmen, when to Æschere's head they
Came on the cliff. The current was seething
With blood and with gore (the troopers gazed on it).
The horn anon sang the battle-song ready.   40
The troop were all seated; they saw 'long the water then
Many a serpent, mere-dragons wondrous

[*The water is filled with serpents and sea-dragons.*]

Trying the waters, nickers a-lying
On the cliffs of the nesses, which at noonday full often
Go on the sea-deeps their sorrowful journey,
Wild-beasts and wormkind; away then they hastened
Hot-mooded, hateful, they heard the great clamor,

[*One of them is killed by Beowulf.*]

The war-trumpet winding. One did the Geat-prince
Sunder from earth-joys, with arrow from bowstring,
From his sea-struggle tore him, that the trusty war-missile   50
Pierced to his vitals; he proved in the currents

[*The dead beast is a poor swimmer.*]

Less doughty at swimming whom death had offcarried.
Soon in the waters the wonderful swimmer
Was straitened most sorely with sword-pointed boar-spears,
Pressed in the battle and pulled to the cliff-edge;
The liegemen then looked on the loath-fashioned stranger.
Beowulf donned then his battle-equipments,

[*Beowulf prepares for a struggle with the monster.*]

Cared little for life; inlaid and most ample,
The hand-woven corslet which could cover his body,
Must the wave-deeps explore, that war might be powerless   60
To harm the great hero, and the hating one's grasp might
Not peril his safety; his head was protected
By the light-flashing helmet that should mix with the bottoms,
Trying the eddies, treasure-emblazoned,
Encircled with jewels, as in seasons long past
The weapon-smith worked it, wondrously made it,
With swine-bodies fashioned it, that thenceforward no longer
Brand might bite it, and battle-sword hurt it.
And that was not least of helpers in prowess
That Hrothgar's spokesman had lent him when straitened;   70

[*He has Unferth's sword in his hand.*]

And the hilted hand-sword was Hrunting entitled,
Old and most excellent 'mong all of the treasures;
Its blade was of iron, blotted with poison,
Hardened with gore; it failed not in battle
Any hero under heaven in hand who it brandished,
Who ventured to take the terrible journeys,
The battle-field sought; not the earliest occasion
That deeds of daring 'twas destined to 'complish.
Ecglaf's kinsman minded not soothly,

[*Unferth has little use for swords.*]

Exulting in strength, what erst he had spoken   80
Drunken with wine, when the weapon he lent to
A sword-hero bolder; himself did not venture
'Neath the strife of the currents his life to endanger,
To fame-deeds perform; there he forfeited glory,
Repute for his strength. Not so with the other
When he clad in his corslet had equipped him for battle.

XXIII. Beowulf's Fight With Grendel's Mother.

Beowulf spake, Ecgtheow's son:

[*Beowulf makes a parting speech to Hrothgar.*]

"Recall now, oh, famous kinsman of Healfdene,
Prince very prudent, now to part I am ready,
Gold-friend of earlmen, what erst we agreed on,
Should I lay down my life in lending thee assistance,

[*If I fail, act as a kind liegelord to my thanes,*

When my earth-joys were over, thou wouldst evermore serve me
In stead of a father; my faithful thanemen,
My trusty retainers, protect thou and care for,
Fall I in battle: and, Hrothgar belovèd,
Send unto Higelac the high-valued jewels   10

and send Higelac the jewels thou hast given me.]

Thou to me hast allotted. The lord of the Geatmen
May perceive from the gold, the Hrethling may see it
When he looks on the jewels, that a gem-giver found I

[*I should like my king to know how generous a lord I found
thee to be.*]

Good over-measure, enjoyed him while able.
And the ancient heirloom Unferth permit thou,
The famed one to have, the heavy-sword splendid[69]
The hard-edgèd weapon; with Hrunting to aid me,
I shall gain me glory, or grim-death shall take me."

---

[69] Kl. emends 'wæl-sweord.' The half-line would then read, '*the battle-sword splendid.*'—For 'heard-ecg' in next half-verse, see note to 20 [39] above.

The atheling of Geatmen uttered these words and

[*Beowulf is eager for the fray.*]

Heroic did hasten, not any rejoinder   20
Was willing to wait for; the wave-current swallowed
The doughty-in-battle. Then a day's-length elapsed ere

[*He is a whole day reaching the bottom of the sea.*]

He was able to see the sea at its bottom.
Early she found then who fifty of winters
The course of the currents kept in her fury,
Grisly and greedy, that the grim one's dominion
Some one of men from above was exploring.

[*Grendel's mother knows that some one has reached her
domains.*]

Forth did she grab them, grappled the warrior
With horrible clutches; yet no sooner she injured
His body unscathèd: the burnie out-guarded,   30
That she proved but powerless to pierce through the armor,
The limb-mail locked, with loath-grabbing fingers.
The sea-wolf bare then, when bottomward came she,
The ring-prince homeward, that he after was powerless

[*She grabs him, and bears him to her den.*]

(He had daring to do it) to deal with his weapons,
But many a mere-beast tormented him swimming,
Flood-beasts no few with fierce-biting tusks did

[*Sea-monsters bite and strike him.*]

Break through his burnie, the brave one pursued they.
The earl then discovered he was down in some cavern
Where no water whatever anywise harmed him,   40
And the clutch of the current could come not anear him,
Since the roofed-hall prevented; brightness a-gleaming
Fire-light he saw, flashing resplendent.
The good one saw then the sea-bottom's monster,
The mighty mere-woman; he made a great onset

[*Beowulf attacks the mother of Grendel.*]

With weapon-of-battle, his hand not desisted
From striking, that war-blade struck on her head then
A battle-song greedy. The stranger perceived then
The sword would not bite, her life would not injure,

[*The sword will not bite.*]

But the falchion failed the folk-prince when straitened: 50
Erst had it often onsets encountered,
Oft cloven the helmet, the fated one's armor:
'Twas the first time that ever the excellent jewel
Had failed of its fame. Firm-mooded after,
Not heedless of valor, but mindful of glory,
Was Higelac's kinsman; the hero-chief angry
Cast then his carved-sword covered with jewels
That it lay on the earth, hard and steel-pointed;
He hoped in his strength, his hand-grapple sturdy.

[*The hero throws down all weapons, and again trusts to his
    hand-grip.*]

So any must act whenever he thinketh   60
To gain him in battle glory unending,
And is reckless of living. The lord of the War-Geats
(He shrank not from battle) seized by the shoulder[70]
The mother of Grendel; then mighty in struggle
Swung he his enemy, since his anger was kindled,
That she fell to the floor. With furious grapple
She gave him requital[71] early thereafter,

[*Beowulf falls.*]

And stretched out to grab him; the strongest of warriors
Faint-mooded stumbled, till he fell in his traces,
Foot-going champion. Then she sat on the hall-guest   70

[*The monster sits on him with drawn sword.*]

---

[70] Sw., R., and t. B. suggest 'feaxe' for 'eaxle' (1538) and render: *Seized by the hair.*
[71] If 'hand-léan' be accepted (as the MS. has it), the line will read: *She hand-reward gave him early thereafter.*

And wielded her war-knife wide-bladed, flashing,
For her son would take vengeance, her one only bairn.
His breast-armor woven bode on his shoulder;

[*His armor saves his life.*]

It guarded his life, the entrance defended
'Gainst sword-point and edges. Ecgtheow's son there
Had fatally journeyed, champion of Geatmen,
In the arms of the ocean, had the armor not given,
Close-woven corslet, comfort and succor,
And had God most holy not awarded the victory,

[*God arranged for his escape.*]

All-knowing Lord; easily did heaven's   80
Ruler most righteous arrange it with justice;[72]
Uprose he erect ready for battle.

XXIV. Beowulf Is Double-Conqueror.

Then he saw mid the war-gems a weapon of victory,

[*Beowulf grasps a giant-sword,*

An ancient giant-sword, of edges a-doughty,
Glory of warriors: of weapons 'twas choicest,
Only 'twas larger than any man else was
Able to bear to the battle-encounter,
The good and splendid work of the giants.
He grasped then the sword-hilt, knight of the Scyldings,
Bold and battle-grim, brandished his ring-sword,
Hopeless of living, hotly he smote her,
That the fiend-woman's neck firmly it grappled,   10
Broke through her bone-joints, the bill fully pierced her

and fells the female monster.]

Fate-cursèd body, she fell to the ground then:
The hand-sword was bloody, the hero exulted.
The brand was brilliant, brightly it glimmered,

---

[72] Sw. and S. change H.-So.'s semicolon (v. 1557) to a comma, and translate: *The Ruler of Heaven arranged it in justice easily, after he arose again.*

Just as from heaven gemlike shineth
The torch of the firmament. He glanced 'long the building,
And turned by the wall then, Higelac's vassal
Raging and wrathful raised his battle-sword
Strong by the handle. The edge was not useless
To the hero-in-battle, but he speedily wished to   20
Give Grendel requital for the many assaults he
Had worked on the West-Danes not once, but often,
When he slew in slumber the subjects of Hrothgar,
Swallowed down fifteen sleeping retainers
Of the folk of the Danemen, and fully as many
Carried away, a horrible prey.
He gave him requital, grim-raging champion,
When he saw on his rest-place weary of conflict

[*Beowulf sees the body of Grendel, and cuts off his head.*]

Grendel lying, of life-joys bereavèd,
As the battle at Heorot erstwhile had scathed him;   30
His body far bounded, a blow when he suffered,
Death having seized him, sword-smiting heavy,
And he cut off his head then. Early this noticed
The clever carles who as comrades of Hrothgar
Gazed on the sea-deeps, that the surging wave-currents

[*The waters are gory.*]

Were mightily mingled, the mere-flood was gory:
Of the good one the gray-haired together held converse,
The hoary of head, that they hoped not to see again

[*Beowulf is given up for dead.*]

The atheling ever, that exulting in victory
He'd return there to visit the distinguished folk-ruler: 40
Then many concluded the mere-wolf had killed him.[73]

---

[73] 'Þæs monige gewearð' (1599) and 'hafað þæs geworden' (2027).—In a paper
published some years ago in one of the Johns Hopkins University circulars, I tried to
throw upon these two long-doubtful passages some light derived from a study of like
passages in Alfred's prose.—The impersonal verb 'geweorðan,' with an accus. of the
person, and a þæt-clause is used several times with the meaning 'agree.' See Orosius
(Sweet's ed.) 178₇; 204₃₄; 208₂₈; 210₁₅; 280₂₀. In the two Beowulf passages, the þæt-
clause is anticipated by 'þæs,' which is clearly a gen. of the thing agreed on.
    The first passage (v. 1599 (b)-1600) I translate literally: *Then many agreed upon
this (namely), that the sea-wolf had killed him.*

The ninth hour came then. From the ness-edge departed
The bold-mooded Scyldings; the gold-friend of heroes
Homeward betook him. The strangers sat down then
Soul-sick, sorrowful, the sea-waves regarding:
They wished and yet weened not their well-loved friend-lord
To see any more. The sword-blade began then,

[*The giant-sword melts.*]

The blood having touched it, contracting and shriveling
With battle-icicles; 'twas a wonderful marvel
That it melted entirely, likest to ice when   50
The Father unbindeth the bond of the frost and
Unwindeth the wave-bands, He who wieldeth dominion
Of times and of tides: a truth-firm Creator.
Nor took he of jewels more in the dwelling,
Lord of the Weders, though they lay all around him,
Than the head and the handle handsome with jewels;
The brand early melted, burnt was the weapon:[74]
So hot was the blood, the strange-spirit poisonous
That in it did perish. He early swam off then

[*The hero swims back to the realms of day.*]

Who had bided in combat the carnage of haters,   60
Went up through the ocean; the eddies were cleansèd,
The spacious expanses, when the spirit from farland
His life put aside and this short-lived existence.
The seamen's defender came swimming to land then
Doughty of spirit, rejoiced in his sea-gift,
The bulky burden which he bore in his keeping.
The excellent vassals advanced then to meet him,
To God they were grateful, were glad in their chieftain,

The second passage (v. 2025 (b)-2027): *She is promised ...*; *to this the friend of the Scyldings has agreed, etc.* By emending 'is' instead of 'wæs' (2025), the tenses will be brought into perfect harmony.

In v. 1997 ff. this same idiom occurs, and was noticed in B.'s great article on Beowulf, which appeared about the time I published my reading of 1599 and 2027. Translate 1997 then: *Wouldst let the South-Danes themselves decide about their struggle with Grendel.* Here 'Súð-Dene' is accus. of person, and 'gúðe' is gen. of thing agreed on.

With such collateral support as that afforded by B. (P. and B. XII. 97), I have no hesitation in departing from H.-So., my usual guide.

The idiom above treated runs through A.-S., Old Saxon, and other Teutonic languages, and should be noticed in the lexicons.

[74] 'Bróden-mæl' is regarded by most scholars as meaning a damaskeened sword. Translate: *The damaskeened sword burned up.* Cf. 25 $_{16}$ and note.

That to see him safe and sound was granted them.
From the high-minded hero, then, helmet and burnie   70
Were speedily loosened: the ocean was putrid,
The water 'neath welkin weltered with gore.
Forth did they fare, then, their footsteps retracing,
Merry and mirthful, measured the earth-way,
The highway familiar: men very daring[75]
Bare then the head from the sea-cliff, burdening
Each of the earlmen, excellent-valiant.
Four of them had to carry with labor

[*It takes four men to carry Grendel's head on a spear.*]

The head of Grendel to the high towering gold-hall
Upstuck on the spear, till fourteen most-valiant   80
And battle-brave Geatmen came there going
Straight to the palace: the prince of the people
Measured the mead-ways, their mood-brave companion.
The atheling of earlmen entered the building,
Deed-valiant man, adorned with distinction,
Doughty shield-warrior, to address King Hrothgar:
Then hung by the hair, the head of Grendel
Was borne to the building, where beer-thanes were drinking,
Loth before earlmen and eke 'fore the lady:
The warriors beheld then a wonderful sight.   90

XXV. Beowulf Brings His Trophies.—Hrothgar's Gratitude.

Beowulf spake, offspring of Ecgtheow:

[*Beowulf relates his last exploit.*]

"Lo! we blithely have brought thee, bairn of Healfdene,
Prince of the Scyldings, these presents from ocean
Which thine eye looketh on, for an emblem of glory.
I came off alive from this, narrowly 'scaping:
In war 'neath the water the work with great pains I
Performed, and the fight had been finished quite nearly,
Had God not defended me. I failed in the battle
Aught to accomplish, aided by Hrunting,
Though that weapon was worthy, but the Wielder of earth-folk   10

---

[75] 'Cyning-balde' (1635) is the much-disputed reading of K. and Th. To render this, *"nobly bold," "excellently bold,"* have been suggested. B. would read 'cyning-holde' (cf. 290), and render: *Men well-disposed towards the king carried the head, etc.* 'Cynebealde,' says t. B., endorsing Gr.

Gave me willingly to see on the wall a

[*God was fighting with me.*]

Heavy old hand-sword hanging in splendor
(He guided most often the lorn and the friendless),
That I swung as a weapon. The wards of the house then
I killed in the conflict (when occasion was given me).
Then the battle-sword burned, the brand that was lifted,[76]
As the blood-current sprang, hottest of war-sweats;
Seizing the hilt, from my foes I offbore it;
I avenged as I ought to their acts of malignity,
The murder of Danemen. I then make thee this promise,   20
Thou'lt be able in Heorot careless to slumber

[*Heorot is freed from monsters.*]

With thy throng of heroes and the thanes of thy people
Every and each, of greater and lesser,
And thou needest not fear for them from the selfsame direction
As thou formerly fearedst, oh, folk-lord of Scyldings,
End-day for earlmen." To the age-hoary man then,
The gray-haired chieftain, the gold-fashioned sword-hilt,

[*The famous sword is presented to Hrothgar.*]

Old-work of giants, was thereupon given;
Since the fall of the fiends, it fell to the keeping
Of the wielder of Danemen, the wonder-smith's labor,   30
And the bad-mooded being abandoned this world then,
Opponent of God, victim of murder,
And also his mother; it went to the keeping
Of the best of the world-kings, where waters encircle,
Who the scot divided in Scylding dominion.
Hrothgar discoursed, the hilt he regarded,

[*Hrothgar looks closely at the old sword.*]

The ancient heirloom where an old-time contention's
Beginning was graven: the gurgling currents,
The flood slew thereafter the race of the giants,
They had proved themselves daring: that people was loth to   40
The Lord everlasting, through lash of the billows

---

[76] Or rather, perhaps, '*the inlaid, or damaskeened weapon.*' Cf. 24 57 and note.

[*It had belonged to a race hateful to God.*]

The Father gave them final requital.
So in letters of rune on the clasp of the handle
Gleaming and golden, 'twas graven exactly,
Set forth and said, whom that sword had been made for,
Finest of irons, who first it was wrought for,
Wreathed at its handle and gleaming with serpents.
The wise one then said (silent they all were)
Son of old Healfdene: "He may say unrefuted

[*Hrothgar praises Beowulf.*]

Who performs 'mid the folk-men fairness and truth   50
(The hoary old ruler remembers the past),
That better by birth is this bairn of the nobles!
Thy fame is extended through far-away countries,
Good friend Beowulf, o'er all of the races,
Thou holdest all firmly, hero-like strength with
Prudence of spirit. I'll prove myself grateful
As before we agreed on; thou granted for long shalt
Become a great comfort to kinsmen and comrades,
A help unto heroes. Heremod became not

[*Heremod's career is again contrasted with Beowulf's.*]

Such to the Scyldings, successors of Ecgwela;   60
He grew not to please them, but grievous destruction,
And diresome death-woes to Danemen attracted;
He slew in anger his table-companions,
Trustworthy counsellors, till he turned off lonely
From world-joys away, wide-famous ruler:
Though high-ruling heaven in hero-strength raised him,
In might exalted him, o'er men of all nations
Made him supreme, yet a murderous spirit
Grew in his bosom: he gave then no ring-gems
To the Danes after custom; endured he unjoyful   70

[*A wretched failure of a king, to give no jewels to his retainers.*]

Standing the straits from strife that was raging,
Longsome folk-sorrow. Learn then from this,
Lay hold of virtue! Though laden with winters,

I have sung thee these measures. 'Tis a marvel to tell it,
How all-ruling God from greatness of spirit

[*Hrothgar moralizes.*]

Giveth wisdom to children of men,
Manor and earlship: all things He ruleth.
He often permitteth the mood-thought of man of
The illustrious lineage to lean to possessions,
Allows him earthly delights at his manor,   80
A high-burg of heroes to hold in his keeping,
Maketh portions of earth-folk hear him,
And a wide-reaching kingdom so that, wisdom failing him,
He himself is unable to reckon its boundaries;
He liveth in luxury, little debars him,
Nor sickness nor age, no treachery-sorrow
Becloudeth his spirit, conflict nowhere,
No sword-hate, appeareth, but all of the world doth
Wend as he wisheth; the worse he knoweth not,
Till arrant arrogance inward pervading,   90
Waxeth and springeth, when the warder is sleeping,
The guard of the soul: with sorrows encompassed,
Too sound is his slumber, the slayer is near him,
Who with bow and arrow aimeth in malice.

XXVI. Hrothgar Moralizes.—Rest After Labor.

"Then bruised in his bosom he with bitter-toothed missile

[*A wounded spirit.*]

Is hurt 'neath his helmet: from harmful pollution
He is powerless to shield him by the wonderful mandates
Of the loath-cursèd spirit; what too long he hath holden
Him seemeth too small, savage he hoardeth,
Nor boastfully giveth gold-plated rings,[77]
The fate of the future flouts and forgetteth
Since God had erst given him greatness no little,
Wielder of Glory. His end-day anear,
It afterward happens that the bodily-dwelling   10
Fleetingly fadeth, falls into ruins;

---

[77] K. says '*proudly giveth.*'—Gr. says, '*And gives no gold-plated rings, in order to incite the recipient to boastfulness.*'—B. suggests 'gyld' for 'gylp,' and renders: *And gives no beaten rings for reward.*

Another lays hold who doleth the ornaments,
The nobleman's jewels, nothing lamenting,
Heedeth no terror. Oh, Beowulf dear,
Best of the heroes, from bale-strife defend thee,
And choose thee the better, counsels eternal;
Beware of arrogance, world-famous champion!

> [*Be not over proud: life is fleeting, and its strength soon*
> *wasteth away.*]

But a little-while lasts thy life-vigor's fulness;
'Twill after hap early, that illness or sword-edge
Shall part thee from strength, or the grasp of the fire,   20
Or the wave of the current, or clutch of the edges,
Or flight of the war-spear, or age with its horrors,
Or thine eyes' bright flashing shall fade into darkness:
'Twill happen full early, excellent hero,
Hrothgar gives an account of his reign.
That death shall subdue thee. So the Danes a half-century
I held under heaven, helped them in struggles
'Gainst many a race in middle-earth's regions,
With ash-wood and edges, that enemies none
On earth molested me. Lo! offsetting change, now,   30
Came to my manor, grief after joyance,

> [*Sorrow after joy.*]

When Grendel became my constant visitor,
Inveterate hater: I from that malice
Continually travailed with trouble no little.
Thanks be to God that I gained in my lifetime,
To the Lord everlasting, to look on the gory
Head with mine eyes, after long-lasting sorrow!
Go to the bench now, battle-adornèd
Joy in the feasting: of jewels in common
We'll meet with many when morning appeareth."   40
The Geatman was gladsome, ganged he immediately
To go to the bench, as the clever one bade him.
Then again as before were the famous-for-prowess,
Hall-inhabiters, handsomely banqueted,
Feasted anew. The night-veil fell then
Dark o'er the warriors. The courtiers rose then;
The gray-haired was anxious to go to his slumbers,
The hoary old Scylding. Hankered the Geatman,
The champion doughty, greatly, to rest him:

[Beowulf is fagged, and seeks rest.]

An earlman early outward did lead him,   50
Fagged from his faring, from far-country springing,
Who for etiquette's sake all of a liegeman's
Needs regarded, such as seamen at that time
Were bounden to feel. The big-hearted rested;
The building uptowered, spacious and gilded,
The guest within slumbered, till the sable-clad raven
Blithely foreboded the beacon of heaven.
Then the bright-shining sun o'er the bottoms came going;[78]
The warriors hastened, the heads of the peoples
Were ready to go again to their peoples,   60
The high-mooded farer would faraway thenceward

[The Geats prepare to leave Dane-land.]

Look for his vessel. The valiant one bade then,[79]
Offspring of Ecglaf, off to bear Hrunting,

*[Unferth asks Beowulf to accept his sword as a gift. Beowulf
thanks him.]*

To take his weapon, his well-beloved iron;
He him thanked for the gift, saying good he accounted
The war-friend and mighty, nor chid he with words then
The blade of the brand: 'twas a brave-mooded hero.
When the warriors were ready, arrayed in their trappings,
The atheling dear to the Danemen advanced then
On to the dais, where the other was sitting,   70
Grim-mooded hero, greeted King Hrothgar.

---

[78] If S.'s emendation be accepted, v. 57 will read: *Then came the light, going bright
after darkness: the warriors, etc.*

[79] As the passage stands in H.-So., Unferth presents Beowulf with the sword
Hrunting, and B. thanks him for the gift. If, however, the suggestions of Grdtvg. and M.
be accepted, the passage will read: *Then the brave one* (i.e. *Beowulf*) *commanded that
Hrunting be borne to the son of Ecglaf* (*Unferth*), *bade him take his sword, his dear
weapon; he* (*B.*) *thanked him* (U.) *for the loan, etc.*

XXVII. Sorrow At Parting.

Beowulf spake, Ecgtheow's offspring:

[*Beowulf's farewell.*]

"We men of the water wish to declare now
Fared from far-lands, we're firmly determined
To seek King Higelac. Here have we fitly
Been welcomed and feasted, as heart would desire it;
Good was the greeting. If greater affection
I am anywise able ever on earth to
Gain at thy hands, ruler of heroes,
Than yet I have done, I shall quickly be ready
For combat and conflict. O'er the course of the waters   10

[*I shall be ever ready to aid thee.*]

Learn I that neighbors alarm thee with terror,
As haters did whilom, I hither will bring thee
For help unto heroes henchmen by thousands.
I know as to Higelac, the lord of the Geatmen,

[*My liegelord will encourage me in aiding thee.*]

Though young in years, he yet will permit me,
By words and by works, ward of the people,
Fully to furnish thee forces and bear thee
My lance to relieve thee, if liegemen shall fail thee,
And help of my hand-strength; if Hrethric be treating,
Bairn of the king, at the court of the Geatmen,   20
He thereat may find him friends in abundance:
Faraway countries he were better to seek for
Who trusts in himself." Hrothgar discoursed then,
Making rejoinder: "These words thou hast uttered
All-knowing God hath given thy spirit!
Ne'er heard I an earlman thus early in life

[*O Beowulf, thou art wise beyond thy years.*]

More clever in speaking: thou'rt cautious of spirit,
Mighty of muscle, in mouth-answers prudent.
I count on the hope that, happen it ever
That missile shall rob thee of Hrethel's descendant,   30

Beowulf

103

Edge-horrid battle, and illness or weapon
Deprive thee of prince, of people's protector,
And life thou yet holdest, the Sea-Geats will never

[*Should Higelac die, the Geats could find no better successor
than thou wouldst make.*]

Find a more fitting folk-lord to choose them,
Gem-ward of heroes, than *thou* mightest prove thee,
If the kingdom of kinsmen thou carest to govern.
Thy mood-spirit likes me the longer the better,
Beowulf dear: thou hast brought it to pass that
To both these peoples peace shall be common,
To Geat-folk and Danemen, the strife be suspended,   40

[*Thou hast healed the ancient breach between our races.*]

The secret assailings they suffered in yore-days;
And also that jewels be shared while I govern
The wide-stretching kingdom, and that many shall visit
Others o'er the ocean with excellent gift-gems:
The ring-adorned bark shall bring o'er the currents
Presents and love-gifts. This people I know
Tow'rd foeman and friend firmly established,[80]
After ancient etiquette everywise blameless."
Then the warden of earlmen gave him still farther,
Kinsman of Healfdene, a dozen of jewels,   50

[*Parting gifts.*]

Bade him safely seek with the presents
His well-beloved people, early returning.
Then the noble-born king kissed the distinguished,

[*Hrothgar kisses Beowulf, and weeps.*]

Dear-lovèd liegeman, the Dane-prince saluted him,
And claspèd his neck; tears from him fell,
From the gray-headed man: he two things expected,
Agèd and reverend, but rather the second,
[81]That bold in council they'd meet thereafter.

---

[80] For 'geworhte,' the crux of this passage, B. proposes 'geþóhte,' rendering: *I know
this people with firm thought every way blameless towards foe and friends.*
[81] S. and B. emend so as to negative the verb 'meet.' "Why should Hrothgar weep if
he expects to meet Beowulf again?" both these scholars ask. But the weeping is

The man was so dear that he failed to suppress the
Emotions that moved him, but in mood-fetters fastened   60
The long-famous hero longeth in secret

[*The old king is deeply grieved to part with his benefactor.*]

Deep in his spirit for the dear-beloved man
Though not a blood-kinsman. Beowulf thenceward,
Gold-splendid warrior, walked o'er the meadows
Exulting in treasure: the sea-going vessel
Riding at anchor awaited its owner.
As they pressed on their way then, the present of Hrothgar
Was frequently referred to: a folk-king indeed that

[*Giving liberally is the true proof of kingship.*]

Everyway blameless, till age did debar him
The joys of his might, which hath many oft injured.   70

XXVIII. The Homeward Journey.—The Two Queens.

Then the band of very valiant retainers
Came to the current; they were clad all in armor,
In link-woven burnies. The land-warder noticed

[*The coast-guard again.*]

The return of the earlmen, as he erstwhile had seen them;
Nowise with insult he greeted the strangers
From the naze of the cliff, but rode on to meet them;
Said the bright-armored visitors[82] vesselward traveled
Welcome to Weders. The wide-bosomed craft then
Lay on the sand, laden with armor,
With horses and jewels, the ring-stemmèd sailer: 10
The mast uptowered o'er the treasure of Hrothgar.
To the boat-ward a gold-bound brand he presented,

[*Beowulf gives the guard a handsome sword.*]

That he was afterwards honored on the ale-bench more highly

---

mentioned before the 'expectations': the tears may have been due to many emotions,
especially gratitude, struggling for expression.

[82] For 'scawan' (1896), 'scaðan' has been proposed. Accepting this, we may render:
He said the bright-armored warriors were going to their vessel, welcome, etc. (Cf. 1804.)

As the heirloom's owner. [83]Set he out on his vessel,
To drive on the deep, Dane-country left he.
Along by the mast then a sea-garment fluttered,
A rope-fastened sail. The sea-boat resounded,
The wind o'er the waters the wave-floater nowise
Kept from its journey; the sea-goer traveled,
The foamy-necked floated forth o'er the currents,   20
The well-fashioned vessel o'er the ways of the ocean,
Till they came within sight of the cliffs of the Geatmen,

[*The Geats see their own land again.*]

The well-known headlands. The wave-goer hastened
Driven by breezes, stood on the shore.
Prompt at the ocean, the port-ward was ready,

[*The port-warden is anxiously looking for them.*]

Who long in the past outlooked in the distance,[84]
At water's-edge waiting well-lovèd heroes;
He bound to the bank then the broad-bosomed vessel
Fast in its fetters, lest the force of the waters
Should be able to injure the ocean-wood winsome.   30
Bade he up then take the treasure of princes,
Plate-gold and fretwork; not far was it thence
To go off in search of the giver of jewels:
Hrethel's son Higelac at home there remaineth,[85]
Himself with his comrades close to the sea-coast.
The building was splendid, the king heroic,
Great in his hall, Hygd very young was,
Fine-mooded, clever, though few were the winters

[*Hygd, the noble queen of Higelac, lavish of gifts.*]

That the daughter of Hæreth had dwelt in the borough;
But she nowise was cringing nor niggard of presents,   40

---

[83] R. suggests, 'Gewát him on naca,' and renders: *The vessel set out, to drive on the sea, the Dane-country left.* 'On' bears the alliteration; cf. 'on hafu' (2524). This has some advantages over the H.-So. reading; viz. (1) It adds nothing to the text; (2) it makes 'naca' the subject, and thus brings the passage into keeping with the context, where the poet has exhausted his vocabulary in detailing the actions of the vessel.—B.'s emendation (cf. P. and B. XII. 97) is violent.

[84] B. translates: *Who for a long time, ready at the coast, had looked out into the distance eagerly for the dear men.* This changes the syntax of 'léofra manna.'

[85] For 'wunað' (v. 1924) several eminent critics suggest 'wunade' (=remained). This makes the passage much clearer.

Of ornaments rare, to the race of the Geatmen.
Thrytho nursed anger, excellent[86] folk-queen,

[*Offa's consort, Thrytho, is contrasted with Hygd.*]

Hot-burning hatred: no hero whatever
'Mong household companions, her husband excepted
Dared to adventure to look at the woman

[*She is a terror to all save her husband.*]

With eyes in the daytime;[87] but he knew that death-chains
Hand-wreathed were wrought him: early thereafter,
When the hand-strife was over, edges were ready,
That fierce-raging sword-point had to force a decision,
Murder-bale show. Such no womanly custom   50
For a lady to practise, though lovely her person,
That a weaver-of-peace, on pretence of anger
A belovèd liegeman of life should deprive.
Soothly this hindered Heming's kinsman;
Other ale-drinking earlmen asserted
That fearful folk-sorrows fewer she wrought them,
Treacherous doings, since first she was given
Adorned with gold to the war-hero youthful,
For her origin honored, when Offa's great palace
O'er the fallow flood by her father's instructions   60
She sought on her journey, where she afterwards fully,
Famed for her virtue, her fate on the king's-seat
Enjoyed in her lifetime, love did she hold with
The ruler of heroes, the best, it is told me,
Of all of the earthmen that oceans encompass,
Of earl-kindreds endless; hence Offa was famous
Far and widely, by gifts and by battles,
Spear-valiant hero; the home of his fathers
He governed with wisdom, whence Eomær did issue
For help unto heroes, Heming's kinsman,   70
Grandson of Garmund, great in encounters.

---

[86] Why should such a woman be described as an 'excellent' queen? C. suggests 'frécnu' = dangerous, bold.

[87] For 'an dæges' various readings have been offered. If 'and-éges' be accepted, the sentence will read: *No hero ... dared look upon her, eye to eye.* If 'án-dæges' be adopted, translate: *Dared look upon her the whole day.*

XXIX. Beowulf and Higelac.

Then the brave one departed, his band along with him,
Seeking the sea-shore, the sea-marches treading,

[*Beowulf and his party seek Higelac.*]

The wide-stretching shores. The world-candle glimmered,
The sun from the southward; they proceeded then onward,
Early arriving where they heard that the troop-lord,
Ongentheow's slayer, excellent, youthful
Folk-prince and warrior was distributing jewels,
Close in his castle. The coming of Beowulf
Was announced in a message quickly to Higelac,
That the folk-troop's defender forth to the palace   10
The linden-companion alive was advancing,
Secure from the combat courtward a-going.
The building was early inward made ready
For the foot-going guests as the good one had ordered.
He sat by the man then who had lived through the struggle,

[*Beowulf sits by his liegelord.*]

Kinsman by kinsman, when the king of the people
Had in lordly language saluted the dear one,
In words that were formal. The daughter of Hæreth

[*Queen Hygd receives the heroes.*]

Coursed through the building, carrying mead-cups:[88]
She loved the retainers, tendered the beakers   20
To the high-minded Geatmen. Higelac 'gan then
Pleasantly plying his companion with questions

[*Higelac is greatly interested in Beowulf's adventures.*]

In the high-towering palace. A curious interest
Tormented his spirit, what meaning to see in
The Sea-Geats' adventures: "Beowulf worthy,
How throve your journeying, when thou thoughtest suddenly

---

[88] 'Meodu-scencum' (1981) some would render '*with mead-pourers.*' Translate then: *The daughter of Hæreth went through the building accompanied by mead-pourers.*

[*Give an account of thy adventures, Beowulf dear.*]

Far o'er the salt-streams to seek an encounter,
A battle at Heorot? Hast bettered for Hrothgar,
The famous folk-leader, his far-published sorrows
Any at all? In agony-billows   30
I mused upon torture, distrusted the journey

[*My suspense has been great.*]

Of the belovèd liegeman; I long time did pray thee
By no means to seek out the murderous spirit,
To suffer the South-Danes themselves to decide on[89]
Grappling with Grendel. To God I am thankful
To be suffered to see thee safe from thy journey."
Beowulf answered, bairn of old Ecgtheow:

[*Beowulf narrates his adventures.*]

"'Tis hidden by no means, Higelac chieftain,
From many of men, the meeting so famous,
What mournful moments of me and of Grendel   40
Were passed in the place where he pressing affliction
On the Victory-Scyldings scathefully brought,
Anguish forever; that all I avengèd,
So that any under heaven of the kinsmen of Grendel
Needeth not boast of that cry-in-the-morning,

[*Grendel's kindred have no cause to boast.*]

Who longest liveth of the loth-going kindred,[90]
Encompassed by moorland. I came in my journey
To the royal ring-hall, Hrothgar to greet there:
Soon did the famous scion of Healfdene,

[*Hrothgar received me very cordially.*]

When he understood fully the spirit that led me,   50
Assign me a seat with the son of his bosom.
The troop was in joyance; mead-glee greater

---

[89] See my note to 1599, supra, and B. in P. and B. XII. 97.
[90] For 'fenne,' supplied by Grdtvg., B. suggests 'fâcne' (cf. Jul. 350). Accepting
this, translate: *Who longest lives of the hated race, steeped in treachery.*

'Neath arch of the ether not ever beheld I
'Mid hall-building holders. The highly-famed queen,

[*The queen also showed up no little honor.*]

Peace-tie of peoples, oft passed through the building,
Cheered the young troopers; she oft tendered a hero
A beautiful ring-band, ere she went to her sitting.
Oft the daughter of Hrothgar in view of the courtiers

[*Hrothgar's lovely daughter.*]

To the earls at the end the ale-vessel carried,
Whom Freaware I heard then hall-sitters title,   60
When nail-adorned jewels she gave to the heroes:
Gold-bedecked, youthful, to the glad son of Froda

[*She is betrothed to Ingeld, in order to unite the Danes and
Heathobards.*]

Her faith has been plighted; the friend of the Scyldings,
The guard of the kingdom, hath given his sanction,[91]
And counts it a vantage, for a part of the quarrels,
A portion of hatred, to pay with the woman.
[92]Somewhere not rarely, when the ruler has fallen,
The life-taking lance relaxeth its fury
For a brief breathing-spell, though the bride be charming!

---

[91] See note to v. 1599 above.

[92] This is perhaps the least understood sentence in the poem, almost every word
being open to dispute. (1) The 'nó' of our text is an emendation, and is rejected by many
scholars. (2) 'Seldan' is by some taken as an adv. (= *seldom*), and by others as a noun (=
page, companion). (3) 'Léod-hryre,' some render '*fall of the people*'; others, '*fall of the
prince.*' (4) 'Búgeð,' most scholars regard as the intrans. verb meaning '*bend,*' '*rest*'; but
one great scholar has translated it '*shall kill.*' (5) 'Hwær,' Very recently, has been
attacked, 'wære' being suggested. (6) As a corollary to the above, the same critic
proposes to drop 'oft' out of the text.—t. B. suggests: Oft seldan wære after léodhryre:
lýtle hwíle bongár búgeð, þéah séo brýd duge = *often has a treaty been (thus) struck,
after a prince had fallen: (but only) a short time is the spear (then) wont to rest, however
excellent the bride may be.*

XXX. *Beowulf Narrates His Adventures to Higelac.*

"It well may discomfit the prince of the Heathobards
And each of the thanemen of earls that attend him,
When he goes to the building escorting the woman,
That a noble-born Daneman the knights should be feasting:
There gleam on his person the leavings of elders
Hard and ring-bright, Heathobards' treasure,
While they wielded their arms, till they misled to the battle
Their own dear lives and belovèd companions.
He saith at the banquet who the collar beholdeth,
An ancient ash-warrior who earlmen's destruction   10
Clearly recalleth (cruel his spirit),
Sadly beginneth sounding the youthful
Thane-champion's spirit through the thoughts of his bosom,
War-grief to waken, and this word-answer speaketh:
'Art thou able, my friend, to know when thou seest it

[*Ingeld is stirred up to break the truce.*]

The brand which thy father bare to the conflict
In his latest adventure, 'neath visor of helmet,
The dearly-loved iron, where Danemen did slay him,
And brave-mooded Scyldings, on the fall of the heroes,
(When vengeance was sleeping) the slaughter-place wielded?   20
E'en now some man of the murderer's progeny
Exulting in ornaments enters the building,
Boasts of his blood-shedding, offbeareth the jewel
Which thou shouldst wholly hold in possession!'
So he urgeth and mindeth on every occasion
With woe-bringing words, till waxeth the season
When the woman's thane for the works of his father,
The bill having bitten, blood-gory sleepeth,
Fated to perish; the other one thenceward
'Scapeth alive, the land knoweth thoroughly.[93]   30
Then the oaths of the earlmen on each side are broken,
When rancors unresting are raging in Ingeld
And his wife-love waxeth less warm after sorrow.
So the Heathobards' favor not faithful I reckon,
Their part in the treaty not true to the Danemen,
Their friendship not fast. I further shall tell thee

---

[93] For 'lifigende' (2063), a mere conjecture, 'wigende' has been suggested. The line
would then read: *Escapeth by fighting, knows the land thoroughly.*

More about Grendel, that thou fully mayst hear,

    [*Having made these preliminary statements, I will now tell
       thee of Grendel, the monster.*]

Ornament-giver, what afterward came from
The hand-rush of heroes. When heaven's bright jewel
O'er earthfields had glided, the stranger came raging,   40
The horrible night-fiend, us for to visit,
Where wholly unharmed the hall we were guarding.
To Hondscio happened a hopeless contention,

    [*Hondscio fell first.*]

Death to the doomed one, dead he fell foremost,
Girded war-champion; to him Grendel became then,
To the vassal distinguished, a tooth-weaponed murderer,
The well-beloved henchman's body all swallowed.
Not the earlier off empty of hand did
The bloody-toothed murderer, mindful of evils,
Wish to escape from the gold-giver's palace,   50
But sturdy of strength he strove to outdo me,
Hand-ready grappled. A glove was suspended
Spacious and wondrous, in art-fetters fastened,
Which was fashioned entirely by touch of the craftman
From the dragon's skin by the devil's devices:
He down in its depths would do me unsadly
One among many, deed-doer raging,
Though sinless he saw me; not so could it happen
When I in my anger upright did stand.
'Tis too long to recount how requital I furnished   60
For every evil to the earlmen's destroyer;
'Twas there, my prince, that I proudly distinguished

    [*I reflected honor upon my people.*]

Thy land with my labors. He left and retreated,
He lived his life a little while longer:
Yet his right-hand guarded his footstep in Heorot,
And sad-mooded thence to the sea-bottom fell he,
Mournful in mind. For the might-rush of battle
The friend of the Scyldings, with gold that was plated,

    [*King Hrothgar lavished gifts upon me.*]

With ornaments many, much requited me,
When daylight had dawned, and down to the banquet   70
We had sat us together. There was chanting and joyance:
The age-stricken Scylding asked many questions
And of old-times related; oft light-ringing harp-strings,
Joy-telling wood, were touched by the brave one;
Now he uttered measures, mourning and truthful,
Then the large-hearted land-king a legend of wonder
Truthfully told us. Now troubled with years
The age-hoary warrior afterward began to

> [*The old king is sad over the loss of his youthful vigor.*]

Mourn for the might that marked him in youth-days;
His breast within boiled, when burdened with winters   80
Much he remembered. From morning till night then
We joyed us therein as etiquette suffered,
Till the second night season came unto earth-folk.
Then early thereafter, the mother of Grendel
Was ready for vengeance, wretched she journeyed;

> [*Grendel's mother.*]

Her son had death ravished, the wrath of the Geatmen.
The horrible woman avengèd her offspring,
And with mighty mainstrength murdered a hero.
There the spirit of Æschere, agèd adviser,

> [*Æschere falls a prey to her vengeance.*]

Was ready to vanish; nor when morn had lightened   90
Were they anywise suffered to consume him with fire,
Folk of the Danemen, the death-weakened hero,
Nor the belovèd liegeman to lay on the pyre;
She the corpse had offcarried in the clutch of the foeman[94]

> [*She suffered not his body to be burned, but ate it.*]

'Neath mountain-brook's flood. To Hrothgar 'twas saddest
Of pains that ever had preyed on the chieftain;
By the life of thee the land-prince then me[95]

---

[94] For 'fæðmum,' Gr.'s conjecture, B. proposes 'færunga.' These three half-verses
would then read: *She bore off the corpse of her foe suddenly under the mountain-torrent.*

Besought very sadly, in sea-currents' eddies
To display my prowess, to peril my safety,
Might-deeds accomplish; much did he promise.   100
I found then the famous flood-current's cruel,

[*I sought the creature in her den,*

Horrible depth-warder. A while unto us two
Hand was in common; the currents were seething
With gore that was clotted, and Grendel's fierce mother's
Head I offhacked in the hall at the bottom

and hewed her head off.]

With huge-reaching sword-edge, hardly I wrested
My life from her clutches; not doomed was I then,
But the warden of earlmen afterward gave me

[*Jewels were freely bestowed upon me.*]

Jewels in quantity, kinsman of Healfdene.

XXXI. Gift-Giving Is Mutual.

"So the belovèd land-prince lived in decorum;
I had missed no rewards, no meeds of my prowess,
But he gave me jewels, regarding my wishes,
Healfdene his bairn; I'll bring them to thee, then,
Atheling of earlmen, offer them gladly.

[*All my gifts I lay at thy feet.*]

And still unto thee is all my affection:[96]
But few of my folk-kin find I surviving
But thee, dear Higelac!" Bade he in then to carry[97]
The boar-image, banner, battle-high helmet,
Iron-gray armor, the excellent weapon,   10

---

[95] The phrase 'þíne lýfe' (2132) was long rendered '*with thy (presupposed) permission.*' The verse would read: *The land-prince then sadly besought me, with thy (presupposed) permission, etc.*

[96] This verse B. renders, '*Now serve I again thee alone as my gracious king.*'

[97] For 'eafor' (2153), Kl. suggests 'ealdor.' Translate then: *Bade the prince then to bear in the banner, battle-high helmet, etc.* On the other hand, W. takes 'eaforhéafodsegn' as a compound, meaning 'helmet': *He bade them bear in the helmet, battle-high helm, gray armor, etc.*

In song-measures said: "This suit-for-the-battle

[*This armor I have belonged of yore to Heregar.*]

Hrothgar presented me, bade me expressly,
Wise-mooded atheling, thereafter to tell thee[98]
The whole of its history, said King Heregar owned it,
Dane-prince for long: yet he wished not to give then
The mail to his son, though dearly he loved him,
Hereward the hardy. Hold all in joyance!"
I heard that there followed hard on the jewels
Two braces of stallions of striking resemblance,
Dappled and yellow; he granted him usance   20
Of horses and treasures. So a kinsman should bear him,
No web of treachery weave for another,
Nor by cunning craftiness cause the destruction
Of trusty companion. Most precious to Higelac,

[*Higelac loves his nephew Beowulf.*]

The bold one in battle, was the bairn of his sister,
And each unto other mindful of favors.
I am told that to Hygd he proffered the necklace,

[*Beowulf gives Hygd the necklace that Wealhtheow had given
him.*]

Wonder-gem rare that Wealhtheow gave him,
The troop-leader's daughter, a trio of horses
Slender and saddle-bright; soon did the jewel   30
Embellish her bosom, when the beer-feast was over.
So Ecgtheow's bairn brave did prove him,
War-famous man, by deeds that were valiant,

[*Beowulf is famous.*]

He lived in honor, belovèd companions
Slew not carousing; his mood was not cruel,
But by hand-strength hugest of heroes then living
The brave one retained the bountiful gift that

---

[98] The H.-So. rendering (ærest = *history, origin*; 'eft' for 'est'), though liable to
objection, is perhaps the best offered. 'That I should very early tell thee of his favor,
kindness' sounds well; but 'his' is badly placed to limit 'est.'—Perhaps, 'eft' with verbs
of saying may have the force of Lat. prefix 're,' and the H.-So. reading mean, 'that I
should its origin rehearse to thee.'

The Lord had allowed him. Long was he wretched,
So that sons of the Geatmen accounted him worthless,
And the lord of the liegemen loth was to do him   40
Mickle of honor, when mead-cups were passing;
They fully believed him idle and sluggish,
An indolent atheling: to the honor-blest man there

[*He is requited for the slights suffered in earlier days.*]

Came requital for the cuts he had suffered.
The folk-troop's defender bade fetch to the building
The heirloom of Hrethel, embellished with gold,
So the brave one enjoined it; there was jewel no richer

[*Higelac overwhelms the conqueror with gifts.*]

In the form of a weapon 'mong Geats of that era;
In Beowulf's keeping he placed it and gave him
Seven of thousands, manor and lordship.   50
Common to both was land 'mong the people,
Estate and inherited rights and possessions,
To the second one specially spacious dominions,
To the one who was better. It afterward happened
In days that followed, befell the battle-thanes,
After Higelac's death, and when Heardred was murdered

[*After Heardred's death, Beowulf becomes king.*]

With weapons of warfare 'neath well-covered targets,
When valiant battlemen in victor-band sought him,
War-Scylfing heroes harassed the nephew
Of Hereric in battle. To Beowulf's keeping   60
Turned there in time extensive dominions:
He fittingly ruled them a fifty of winters

[*He rules the Geats fifty years.*]

(He a man-ruler wise was, manor-ward old) till
A certain one 'gan, on gloom-darkening nights, a
Dragon, to govern, who guarded a treasure,

[*The fire-drake.*]

A high-rising stone-cliff, on heath that was grayish:
A path 'neath it lay, unknown unto mortals.
Some one of earthmen entered the mountain,
The heathenish hoard laid hold of with ardor;
*   *   *   *   *   *   *   70
*   *   *   *   *   *   *
*   *   *   *   *   *   *
*   *   *   *   *   *   *
*   *   *   *   *   *   *

XXXII. The Hoard and the Dragon.

*   *   *   *   *   *   *

He sought of himself who sorely did harm him,
But, for need very pressing, the servant of one of
The sons of the heroes hate-blows evaded,
Seeking for shelter and the sin-driven warrior
Took refuge within there. He early looked in it,
*   *   *   *   *   *   *
*   *   *   *   *   *   *
*   *   *   *   *   when the onset surprised him,
He a gem-vessel saw there: many of suchlike   10

[*The hoard.*]

Ancient ornaments in the earth-cave were lying,
As in days of yore some one of men of
Illustrious lineage, as a legacy monstrous,
There had secreted them, careful and thoughtful,
Dear-valued jewels. Death had offsnatched them,
In the days of the past, and the one man moreover
Of the flower of the folk who fared there the longest,
Was fain to defer it, friend-mourning warder,
A little longer to be left in enjoyment
Of long-lasting treasure.[99] A barrow all-ready   20
Stood on the plain the stream-currents nigh to,
New by the ness-edge, unnethe of approaching:
The keeper of rings carried within a
[100]Ponderous deal of the treasure of nobles,

---

[99] For 'long-gestréona,' B. suggests 'láengestréona,' and renders, *Of fleeting treasures.* S. accepts H.'s 'long-gestréona,' but renders, *The treasure long in accumulating.*

Of gold that was beaten, briefly he spake then:[101]
"Hold thou, O Earth, now heroes no more may,

[*The ring-giver bewails the loss of retainers.*]

The earnings of earlmen. Lo! erst in thy bosom
Worthy men won them; war-death hath ravished,
Perilous life-bale, all my warriors,
Liegemen belovèd, who this life have forsaken,   30
Who hall-pleasures saw. No sword-bearer have I,
And no one to burnish the gold-plated vessel,
The high-valued beaker: my heroes are vanished.
The hardy helmet behung with gilding
Shall be reaved of its riches: the ring-cleansers slumber
Who were charged to have ready visors-for-battle,
And the burnie that bided in battle-encounter
O'er breaking of war-shields the bite of the edges
Moulds with the hero. The ring-twisted armor,
Its lord being lifeless, no longer may journey   40
Hanging by heroes; harp-joy is vanished,
The rapture of glee-wood, no excellent falcon
Swoops through the building, no swift-footed charger
Grindeth the gravel. A grievous destruction
No few of the world-folk widely hath scattered!"
So, woful of spirit one after all
Lamented mournfully, moaning in sadness
By day and by night, till death with its billows
Dashed on his spirit. Then the ancient dusk-scather

[*The fire-dragon.*]

Found the great treasure standing all open,   50
He who flaming and fiery flies to the barrows,
Naked war-dragon, nightly escapeth
Encompassed with fire; men under heaven
Widely beheld him. 'Tis said that he looks for[102]
The hoard in the earth, where old he is guarding
The heathenish treasure; he'll be nowise the better.

---

[100] For 'hard-fyrdne' (2246), B. first suggested 'hard-fyndne,' rendering: *A heap of treasures ... so great that its equal would be hard to find.* The same scholar suggests later 'hord-wynne dæl' = *A deal of treasure-joy.*

[101] Some read 'fec-word' (2247), and render: *Banning words uttered.*

[102] An earlier reading of H.'s gave the following meaning to this passage: *He is said to inhabit a mound under the earth, where he, etc.* The translation in the text is more authentic.

So three-hundred winters the waster of peoples

[*The dragon meets his match.*]

Held upon earth that excellent hoard-hall,
Till the forementioned earlman angered him bitterly:
The beat-plated beaker he bare to his chieftain   60
And fullest remission for all his remissness
Begged of his liegelord. Then the hoard[103] was discovered,
The treasure was taken, his petition was granted
The lorn-mooded liegeman. His lord regarded

[*The hero plunders the dragon's den.*]

The old-work of earth-folk—'twas the earliest occasion.
When the dragon awoke, the strife was renewed there;
He snuffed 'long the stone then, stout-hearted found he
The footprint of foeman; too far had he gone
With cunning craftiness close to the head of
The fire-spewing dragon. So undoomed he may 'scape from   70
Anguish and exile with ease who possesseth
The favor of Heaven. The hoard-warden eagerly
Searched o'er the ground then, would meet with the person
That caused him sorrow while in slumber reclining:
Gleaming and wild he oft went round the cavern,
All of it outward; not any of earthmen
Was seen in that desert.[104] Yet he joyed in the battle,
Rejoiced in the conflict: oft he turned to the barrow,
Sought for the gem-cup;[105] this he soon perceived then
That some man or other had discovered the gold,   80

[*The dragon perceives that some one has disturbed his
treasure.*]

The famous folk-treasure. Not fain did the hoard-ward
Wait until evening; then the ward of the barrow
Was angry in spirit, the loathèd one wished to

---

[103] The repetition of 'hord' in this passage has led some scholars to suggest new readings to avoid the second 'hord.' This, however, is not under the main stress, and, it seems to me, might easily be accepted.

[104] The reading of H.-So. is well defended in the notes to that volume. B. emends and renders: *Nor was there any man in that desert who rejoiced in conflict, in battle-work.* That is, the hoard-ward could not find any one who had disturbed his slumbers, for no warrior was there, t. B.'s emendation would give substantially the same translation.

[105] 'Sinc-fæt' (2301): this word both here and in v. 2232, t. B. renders 'treasure.'

Pay for the dear-valued drink-cup with fire.
Then the day was done as the dragon would have it,
He no longer would wait on the wall, but departed
Fire-impelled, flaming. Fearful the start was

[*The dragon is infuriated.*]

To earls in the land, as it early thereafter
To their giver-of-gold was grievously ended.

XXXIII. Brave Though Aged.—Reminiscences.

The stranger began then to vomit forth fire,

[*The dragon spits fire.*]

To burn the great manor; the blaze then glimmered
For anguish to earlmen, not anything living
Was the hateful air-goer willing to leave there.
The war of the worm widely was noticed,
The feud of the foeman afar and anear,
How the enemy injured the earls of the Geatmen,
Harried with hatred: back he hied to the treasure,
To the well-hidden cavern ere the coming of daylight.
He had circled with fire the folk of those regions,   10
With brand and burning; in the barrow he trusted,
In the wall and his war-might: the weening deceived him.
Then straight was the horror to Beowulf published,

[*Beowulf hears of the havoc wrought by the dragon.*]

Early forsooth, that his own native homestead,[106]
The best of buildings, was burning and melting,
Gift-seat of Geatmen. 'Twas a grief to the spirit
Of the good-mooded hero, the greatest of sorrows:
The wise one weened then that wielding his kingdom

[*He fears that Heaven is punishing him for some crime.*]

'Gainst the ancient commandments, he had bitterly angered
The Lord everlasting: with lorn meditations   20
His bosom welled inward, as was nowise his custom.
The fire-spewing dragon fully had wasted

---

[106] 'Hám' (2326), the suggestion of B. is accepted by t. B. and other scholars.

The fastness of warriors, the water-land outward,
The manor with fire. The folk-ruling hero,
Prince of the Weders, was planning to wreak him.
The warmen's defender bade them to make him,
Earlmen's atheling, an excellent war-shield
Wholly of iron: fully he knew then

  [*He orders an iron shield to be made from him, wood is
  useless.*]

That wood from the forest was helpless to aid him,
Shield against fire. The long-worthy ruler   30
Must live the last of his limited earth-days,
Of life in the world and the worm along with him,
Though he long had been holding hoard-wealth in plenty.
Then the ring-prince disdained to seek with a war-band,

  [*He determines to fight alone.*]

With army extensive, the air-going ranger;
He felt no fear of the foeman's assaults and
He counted for little the might of the dragon,
His power and prowess: for previously dared he
A heap of hostility, hazarded dangers,

  [*Beowulf's early triumphs referred to.*]

War-thane, when Hrothgar's palace he cleansèd,   40
Conquering combatant, clutched in the battle
The kinsmen of Grendel, of kindred detested.[107]
'Twas of hand-fights not least where Higelac was slaughtered,

  [*Higelac's death recalled.*]

When the king of the Geatmen with clashings of battle,
Friend-lord of folks in Frisian dominions,
Offspring of Hrethrel perished through sword-drink,
With battle-swords beaten; thence Beowulf came then
On self-help relying, swam through the waters;
He bare on his arm, lone-going, thirty
Outfits of armor, when the ocean he mounted.   50
The Hetwars by no means had need to be boastful

---

[107] For 'láðan cynnes' (2355), t. B. suggests 'láðan cynne,' apposition to 'mægum.'
From syntactical and other considerations, this is a most excellent emendation.

Of their fighting afoot, who forward to meet him
Carried their war-shields: not many returned from
The brave-mooded battle-knight back to their homesteads.
Ecgtheow's bairn o'er the bight-courses swam then,
Lone-goer lorn to his land-folk returning,
Where Hygd to him tendered treasure and kingdom,
Rings and dominion: her son she not trusted,

[*Heardred's lack of capacity to rule.*]

To be able to keep the kingdom devised him
'Gainst alien races, on the death of King Higelac.   60
Yet the sad ones succeeded not in persuading the atheling

[*Beowulf's tact and delicacy recalled.*]

In any way ever, to act as a suzerain
To Heardred, or promise to govern the kingdom;
Yet with friendly counsel in the folk he sustained him,
Gracious, with honor, till he grew to be older,
Wielded the Weders. Wide-fleeing outlaws,

[*Reference is here made to a visit which Beowulf receives
from Eanmund and Eadgils, why they come is not known.*]

Ohthere's sons, sought him o'er the waters:
They had stirred a revolt 'gainst the helm of the Scylfings,
The best of the sea-kings, who in Swedish dominions
Distributed treasure, distinguished folk-leader.   70
'Twas the end of his earth-days; injury fatal[108]
By swing of the sword he received as a greeting,
Offspring of Higelac; Ongentheow's bairn
Later departed to visit his homestead,
When Heardred was dead; let Beowulf rule them,
Govern the Geatmen: good was that folk-king.

XXXIV. Beowulf Seeks the Dragon.—Beowulf's Reminiscences.

He planned requital for the folk-leader's ruin
In days thereafter, to Eadgils the wretched
Becoming an enemy. Ohthere's son then
Went with a war-troop o'er the wide-stretching currents

---

[108] Gr. read 'on feorme' (2386), rendering: *He there at the banquet a fatal wound received by blows of the sword.*

With warriors and weapons: with woe-journeys cold he
After avenged him, the king's life he took.
So he came off uninjured from all of his battles,

[*Beowulf has been preserved through many perils.*]

Perilous fights, offspring of Ecgtheow,
From his deeds of daring, till that day most momentous
When he fate-driven fared to fight with the dragon.   10
With eleven companions the prince of the Geatmen

[*With eleven comrades, he seeks the dragon.*]

Went lowering with fury to look at the fire-drake:
Inquiring he'd found how the feud had arisen,
Hate to his heroes; the highly-famed gem-vessel
Was brought to his keeping through the hand of th' informer.
That in the throng was thirteenth of heroes,

[*A guide leads the way, but...*]

That caused the beginning of conflict so bitter,
Captive and wretched, must sad-mooded thenceward
Point out the place: he passed then unwillingly

...very reluctantly.]

To the spot where he knew of the notable cavern,   20
The cave under earth, not far from the ocean,
The anger of eddies, which inward was full of
Jewels and wires: a warden uncanny,
Warrior weaponed, wardered the treasure,
Old under earth; no easy possession
For any of earth-folk access to get to.
Then the battle-brave atheling sat on the naze-edge,
While the gold-friend of Geatmen gracious saluted
His fireside-companions: woe was his spirit,
Death-boding, wav'ring; Weird very near him,   30
Who must seize the old hero, his soul-treasure look for,
Dragging aloof his life from his body:
Not flesh-hidden long was the folk-leader's spirit.
Beowulf spake, Ecgtheow's son:
"I survived in my youth-days many a conflict,

[*Beowulf's retrospect.*]

Hours of onset: that all I remember.
I was seven-winters old when the jewel-prince took me,
High-lord of heroes, at the hands of my father,
Hrethel the hero-king had me in keeping,
Gave me treasure and feasting, our kinship remembered;   40

[*Hrethel took me when I was seven.*]

Not ever was I *any* less dear to him
Knight in the boroughs, than the bairns of his household,

[*He treated me as a son.*]

Herebald and Hæthcyn and Higelac mine.
To the eldest unjustly by acts of a kinsman
Was murder-bed strewn, since him Hæthcyn from horn-bow
His sheltering chieftain shot with an arrow,

[*One of the brothers accidentally kills another.*]

Erred in his aim and injured his kinsman,
One brother the other, with blood-sprinkled spear:
'Twas a feeless fight, finished in malice,

[*No fee could compound for such a calamity.*]

Sad to his spirit; the folk-prince however   50
Had to part from existence with vengeance untaken.
So to hoar-headed hero 'tis heavily crushing[109]

[*A parallel case is supposed.*]

---

[109] 'Gomelum ceorle' (2445).—H. takes these words as referring to Hrethel; but the translator here departs from his editor by understanding the poet to refer to a hypothetical old man, introduced as an illustration of a father's sorrow.

Hrethrel had certainly never seen a son of his ride on the gallows to feed the crows. The passage beginning 'swá bið géomorlic' seems to be an effort to reach a full simile, 'as ... so.' 'As it is mournful for an old man, etc. ... so the defence of the Weders (2463) bore heart-sorrow, etc.' The verses 2451 to 2463½ would be parenthetical, the poet's feelings being so strong as to interrupt the simile. The punctuation of the fourth edition would be better—a comma after 'galgan' (2447). The translation may be indicated as follows: (*Just*) *as it is sad for an old man to see his son ride young on the gallows when he himself is uttering mournful measures, a sorrowful song, while his son hangs for a comfort to the raven, and he, old and infirm, cannot render him any kelp—* (*he is constantly reminded, etc.*, 2451-2463)—*so the defence of the Weders, etc.*

To live to see his son as he rideth
Young on the gallows: then measures he chanteth,
A song of sorrow, when his son is hanging
For the raven's delight, and aged and hoary
He is unable to offer any assistance.
Every morning his offspring's departure
Is constant recalled: he cares not to wait for
The birth of an heir in his borough-enclosures,   60
Since that one through death-pain the deeds hath experienced.
He heart-grieved beholds in the house of his son the
Wine-building wasted, the wind-lodging places
Reaved of their roaring; the riders are sleeping,
The knights in the grave; there's no sound of the harp-wood,
Joy in the yards, as of yore were familiar.

XXXV. Reminiscences (continued).—Beowulf's Last Battle.

"He seeks then his chamber, singeth a woe-song
One for the other; all too extensive
Seemed homesteads and plains. So the helm of the Weders
Mindful of Herebald heart-sorrow carried,

[*Hrethel grieves for Herebald.*]

Stirred with emotion, nowise was able
To wreak his ruin on the ruthless destroyer:
He was unable to follow the warrior with hatred,
With deeds that were direful, though dear he not held him.
Then pressed by the pang this pain occasioned him,
He gave up glee, God-light elected;   10
He left to his sons, as the man that is rich does,
His land and fortress, when from life he departed.
Then was crime and hostility 'twixt Swedes and Geatmen,

[*Strife between Swedes and Geats.*]

O'er wide-stretching water warring was mutual,
Burdensome hatred, when Hrethel had perished,
And Ongentheow's offspring were active and valiant,
Wished not to hold to peace oversea, but
Round Hreosna-beorh often accomplished
Cruelest massacre. This my kinsman avengèd,
The feud and fury, as 'tis found on inquiry,   20
Though one of them paid it with forfeit of life-joys,
With price that was hard: the struggle became then

[*Hæthcyn's fall at Ravenswood.*]

Fatal to Hæthcyn, lord of the Geatmen.
Then I heard that at morning one brother the other
With edges of irons egged on to murder,
Where Ongentheow maketh onset on Eofor:
The helmet crashed, the hoary-haired Scylfing
Sword-smitten fell, his hand then remembered
Feud-hate sufficient, refused not the death-blow.
The gems that he gave me, with jewel-bright sword I   30

[*I requited him for the jewels he gave me.*]

'Quited in contest, as occasion was offered:
Land he allowed me, life-joy at homestead,
Manor to live on. Little he needed
From Gepids or Danes or in Sweden to look for
Trooper less true, with treasure to buy him;
'Mong foot-soldiers ever in front I would hie me,
Alone in the vanguard, and evermore gladly
Warfare shall wage, while this weapon endureth
That late and early often did serve me
When I proved before heroes the slayer of Dæghrefn,   40

[*Beowulf refers to his having slain Dæghrefn.*]

Knight of the Hugmen: he by no means was suffered
To the king of the Frisians to carry the jewels,
The breast-decoration; but the banner-possessor
Bowed in the battle, brave-mooded atheling.
No weapon was slayer, but war-grapple broke then
The surge of his spirit, his body destroying.
Now shall weapon's edge make war for the treasure,
And hand and firm-sword." Beowulf spake then,
Boast-words uttered—the latest occasion:
"I braved in my youth-days battles unnumbered;   50

[*He boasts of his youthful prowess, and declares himself still
    fearless.*]

Still am I willing the struggle to look for,
Fame-deeds perform, folk-warden prudent,
If the hateful despoiler forth from his cavern
Seeketh me out!" Each of the heroes,

Helm-bearers sturdy, he thereupon greeted
Belovèd co-liegemen—his last salutation:

[*His last salutations.*]

"No brand would I bear, no blade for the dragon,
Wist I a way my word-boast to 'complish[110]
Else with the monster, as with Grendel I did it;
But fire in the battle hot I expect there,   60
Furious flame-burning: so I fixed on my body
Target and war-mail. The ward of the barrow[111]
I'll not flee from a foot-length, the foeman uncanny.
At the wall 'twill befall us as Fate decreeth,
Each one's Creator. I am eager in spirit,

[*Let Fate decide between us.*]

With the wingèd war-hero to away with all boasting.
Bide on the barrow with burnies protected,
Earls in armor, which of *us* two may better

[*Wait ye here till the battle is over.*]

Bear his disaster, when the battle is over.
'Tis no matter of yours, and man cannot do it,   70
But me and me only, to measure his strength with
The monster of malice, might-deeds to 'complish.
I with prowess shall gain the gold, or the battle,
Direful death-woe will drag off your ruler!"
The mighty champion rose by his shield then,
Brave under helmet, in battle-mail went he
'Neath steep-rising stone-cliffs, the strength he relied on
Of one man alone: no work for a coward.
Then he saw by the wall who a great many battles
Had lived through, most worthy, when foot-troops collided,   80
Stone-arches standing, stout-hearted champion,

[*The place of strife is described.*]

Saw a brook from the barrow bubbling out thenceward:

---

[110] The clause 2520(2)-2522(1), rendered by 'Wist I … monster,' Gr., followed by
S., translates substantially as follows: *If I knew how else I might combat the boastful
defiance of the monster.*—The translation turns upon 'wiðgrípan,' a word not understood.
[111] B. emends and translates: *I will not flee the space of a foot from the guard of the
barrow, but there shall be to us a fight at the wall, as fate decrees, each one's Creator.*

The flood of the fountain was fuming with war-flame:
Not nigh to the hoard, for season the briefest
Could he brave, without burning, the abyss that was yawning,
The drake was so fiery. The prince of the Weders
Caused then that words came from his bosom,
So fierce was his fury; the firm-hearted shouted:
His battle-clear voice came in resounding
'Neath the gray-colored stone. Stirred was his hatred,   90
The hoard-ward distinguished the speech of a man;

[*Beowulf calls out under the stone arches.*]

Time was no longer to look out for friendship.
The breath of the monster issued forth first,
Vapory war-sweat, out of the stone-cave:
The earth re-echoed. The earl 'neath the barrow

[*The terrible encounter.*]

Lifted his shield, lord of the Geatmen,
Tow'rd the terrible stranger: the ring-twisted creature's
Heart was then ready to seek for a struggle.
The excellent battle-king first brandished his weapon,

[*Beowulf brandishes his sword,*

The ancient heirloom, of edges unblunted,[112]   100
To the death-planners twain was terror from other.
The lord of the troopers intrepidly stood then

and stands against his shield.]

'Gainst his high-rising shield, when the dragon coiled him
Quickly together: in corslet he bided.

[*The dragon coils himself.*]

He went then in blazes, bended and striding,
Hasting him forward. His life and body
The targe well protected, for time-period shorter
Than wish demanded for the well-renowned leader,

---

[112] The translation of this passage is based on 'unsláw' (2565), accepted by H.-So., in lieu of the long-standing 'ungléaw.' The former is taken as an adj. limiting 'sweord'; the latter as an adj. c. 'gúð-cyning': *The good war-king, rash with edges, brandished his sword, his old relic.* The latter gives a more rhetorical Anglo-Saxon (poetical) sentence.

Where he then for the first day was forced to be victor,
Famous in battle, as Fate had not willed it.   110
The lord of the Geatmen uplifted his hand then,
Smiting the fire-drake with sword that was precious,
That bright on the bone the blade-edge did weaken,
Bit more feebly than his folk-leader needed,
Burdened with bale-griefs. Then the barrow-protector,
When the sword-blow had fallen, was fierce in his spirit,

[*The dragon rages.*]

Flinging his fires, flamings of battle
Gleamed then afar: the gold-friend of Weders
Boasted no conquests, his battle-sword failed him

[*Beowulf's sword fails him.*]

Naked in conflict, as by no means it ought to,   120
Long-trusty weapon. 'Twas no slight undertaking
That Ecgtheow's famous offspring would leave
The drake-cavern's bottom; he must live in some region
Other than this, by the will of the dragon,
As each one of earthmen existence must forfeit.
'Twas early thereafter the excellent warriors
Met with each other. Anew and afresh

[*The combat is renewed.*]

The hoard-ward took heart (gasps heaved then his bosom):
Sorrow he suffered encircled with fire

[*The great hero is reduced to extremities.*]

Who the people erst governed. His companions by no means   130
Were banded about him, bairns of the princes,
With valorous spirit, but they sped to the forest,

[*His comrades flee!*]

Seeking for safety. The soul-deeps of one were
Ruffled by care: kin-love can never

[*Blood is thicker than water.*]

Aught in him waver who well doth consider.

XXXVI. Wiglaf the Trusty.—Beowulf Is Deserted By Friends and By Sword.

The son of Weohstan was Wiglaf entitled,

[Wiglaf remains true—the ideal Teutonic liegeman.]

Shield-warrior precious, prince of the Scylfings,
Ælfhere's kinsman: he saw his dear liegelord
Enduring the heat 'neath helmet and visor.
Then he minded the holding that erst he had given him,
The Wægmunding warriors' wealth-blessèd homestead,

[Wiglaf recalls Beowulf's generosity.]

Each of the folk-rights his father had wielded;
He was hot for the battle, his hand seized the target,
The yellow-bark shield, he unsheathed his old weapon,
Which was known among earthmen as the relic of Eanmund,   10
Ohthere's offspring, whom, exiled and friendless,
Weohstan did slay with sword-edge in battle,
And carried his kinsman the clear-shining helmet,
The ring-made burnie, the old giant-weapon
That Onela gave him, his boon-fellow's armor,
Ready war-trappings: he the feud did not mention,
Though he'd fatally smitten the son of his brother.
Many a half-year held he the treasures,
The bill and the burnie, till his bairn became able,
Like his father before him, fame-deeds to 'complish;   20
Then he gave him 'mong Geatmen a goodly array of
Weeds for his warfare; he went from life then
Old on his journey. 'Twas the earliest time then
That the youthful champion might charge in the battle

[This is Wiglaf's first battle as liegeman of Beowulf.]

Aiding his liegelord; his spirit was dauntless.
Nor did kinsman's bequest quail at the battle:
This the dragon discovered on their coming together.
Wiglaf uttered many a right-saying,
Said to his fellows, sad was his spirit:
"I remember the time when, tasting the mead-cup,   30

[Wiglaf appeals to the pride of the cowards.]

We promised in the hall the lord of us all
Who gave us these ring-treasures, that this battle-equipment,
Swords and helmets, we'd certainly quite him,
Should need of such aid ever befall him:
In the war-band he chose us for this journey spontaneously,

[*How we have forfeited our liegelord's confidence!*]

Stirred us to glory and gave me these jewels,
Since he held and esteemed us trust-worthy spearmen,
Hardy helm-bearers, though this hero-achievement
Our lord intended alone to accomplish,
Ward of his people, for most of achievements,   40
Doings audacious, he did among earth-folk.
The day is now come when the ruler of earthmen

[*Our lord is in sore need of us.*]

Needeth the vigor of valiant heroes:
Let us wend us towards him, the war-prince to succor,
While the heat yet rageth, horrible fire-fight.
God wot in me, 'tis mickle the liefer

[*I would rather die than go home with out my suzerain.*]

The blaze should embrace my body and eat it
With my treasure-bestower. Meseemeth not proper
To bear our battle-shields back to our country,
'Less first we are able to fell and destroy the   50
Long-hating foeman, to defend the life of
The prince of the Weders. Well do I know 'tisn't

[*Surely he does not deserve to die alone.*]

Earned by his exploits, he only of Geatmen
Sorrow should suffer, sink in the battle:
Brand and helmet to us both shall be common,
[113]Shield-cover, burnie." Through the bale-smoke he stalked then,

---

[113] The passage '*Brand ... burnie,*' is much disputed. In the first place, some eminent critics assume a gap of at least two half-verses.—'Úrum' (2660), being a peculiar form, has been much discussed. 'Byrdu-scrúd' is also a crux. B. suggests 'býwdu-scrúd' = *splendid vestments.* Nor is 'bám' accepted by all, 'béon' being suggested. Whatever the individual words, the passage must mean, "*I intend to share with him my equipments of defence.*"

Went under helmet to the help of his chieftain,
Briefly discoursing: "Beowulf dear,

[*Wiglaf reminds Beowulf of his youthful boasts.*]

Perform thou all fully, as thou formerly saidst,
In thy youthful years, that while yet thou livedst   60
Thou wouldst let thine honor not ever be lessened.
Thy life thou shalt save, mighty in actions,
Atheling undaunted, with all of thy vigor;
I'll give thee assistance." The dragon came raging,

[*The monster advances on them.*]

Wild-mooded stranger, when these words had been uttered
('Twas the second occasion), seeking his enemies,
Men that were hated, with hot-gleaming fire-waves;
With blaze-billows burned the board to its edges:
The fight-armor failed then to furnish assistance
To the youthful spear-hero: but the young-agèd stripling   70
Quickly advanced 'neath his kinsman's war-target,
Since his own had been ground in the grip of the fire.
Then the warrior-king was careful of glory,

[*Beowulf strikes at the dragon.*]

He soundly smote with sword-for-the-battle,
That it stood in the head by hatred driven;
Nægling was shivered, the old and iron-made
Brand of Beowulf in battle deceived him.

[*His sword fails him.*]

'Twas denied him that edges of irons were able
To help in the battle; the hand was too mighty
[114]Which every weapon, as I heard on inquiry,   80
Outstruck in its stroke, when to struggle he carried
The wonderful war-sword: it waxed him no better.
Then the people-despoiler—third of his onsets—

[*The dragon advances on Beowulf again.*]

---

[114] B. would render: *Which, as I heard, excelled in stroke every sword that he carried to the strife, even the strongest (sword)*. For 'Þonne' he reads 'Þone,' rel. pr.

Fierce-raging fire-drake, of feud-hate was mindful,
Charged on the strong one, when chance was afforded,
Heated and war-grim, seized on his neck
With teeth that were bitter; he bloody did wax with
Soul-gore seething; sword-blood in waves boiled.

XXXVII. The Fatal Struggle.—Beowulf's Last Moments.

Then I heard that at need of the king of the people

[*Wiglaf defends Beowulf.*]

The upstanding earlman exhibited prowess,
Vigor and courage, as suited his nature;
[115]He his head did not guard, but the high-minded liegeman's
Hand was consumed, when he succored his kinsman,
So he struck the strife-bringing strange-comer lower,
Earl-thane in armor, that *in* went the weapon
Gleaming and plated, that 'gan then the fire[116]
Later to lessen. The liegelord himself then

[*Beowulf draws his knife,...*

Retained his consciousness, brandished his war-knife,   10
Battle-sharp, bitter, that he bare on his armor:
The Weder-lord cut the worm in the middle.

...and cuts the dragon.]

They had felled the enemy (life drove out then[117]
Puissant prowess), the pair had destroyed him,
Land-chiefs related: so a liegeman should prove him,
A thaneman when needed. To the prince 'twas the last of
His era of conquest by his own great achievements,

---

[115] B. renders: *He (W.) did not regard his (the dragon's) head* (since Beowulf had struck it without effect), *but struck the dragon a little lower down.*—One crux is to find out whose head is meant; another is to bring out the antithesis between 'head' and 'hand.'

[116] 'þæt þæt fýr' (2702), S. emends to 'þá þæt fýr' = *when the fire began to grow less intense afterward.* This emendation relieves the passage of a plethora of conjunctive þæt's.

[117] For 'gefyldan' (2707), S. proposes 'gefylde.' The passage would read: *He felled the foe (life drove out strength), and they then both had destroyed him, chieftains related.* This gives Beowulf the credit of having felled the dragon; then they combine to annihilate him.— For 'ellen' (2707), Kl. suggests 'e(a)llne.'—The reading '*life drove out strength*' is very unsatisfactory and very peculiar. I would suggest as follows: Adopt S.'s emendation, remove H.'s parenthesis, read 'ferh-ellen wræc,' and translate: *He felled the foe, drove out his life-strength* (that is, made him *hors de combat*), *and then they both, etc.*

The latest of world-deeds. The wound then began

[*Beowulf's wound swells and burns.*]

Which the earth-dwelling dragon erstwhile had wrought him
To burn and to swell. He soon then discovered   20
That bitterest bale-woe in his bosom was raging,
Poison within. The atheling advanced then,
That along by the wall, he prudent of spirit

[*He sits down exhausted.*]

Might sit on a settle; he saw the giant-work,
How arches of stone strengthened with pillars
The earth-hall eternal inward supported.
Then the long-worthy liegeman laved with his hand the
Far-famous chieftain, gory from sword-edge,

[*Wiglaf bathes his lord's head.*]

Refreshing the face of his friend-lord and ruler,
Sated with battle, unbinding his helmet.   30
Beowulf answered, of his injury spake he,
His wound that was fatal (he was fully aware
He had lived his allotted life-days enjoying
The pleasures of earth; then past was entirely
His measure of days, death very near):
"My son I would give now my battle-equipments,

[*Beowulf regrets that he has no son.*]

Had any of heirs been after me granted,
Along of my body. This people I governed
Fifty of winters: no king 'mong my neighbors
Dared to encounter me with comrades-in-battle,   40
Try me with terror. The time to me ordered
I bided at home, mine own kept fitly,
Sought me no snares, swore me not many
Oaths in injustice. Joy over all this

[*I can rejoice in a well-spent life.*]

I'm able to have, though ill with my death-wounds;
Hence the Ruler of Earthmen need not charge me
With the killing of kinsmen, when cometh my life out

Forth from my body. Fare thou with haste now
To behold the hoard 'neath the hoar-grayish stone,

> [*Bring me the hoard, Wiglaf, that my dying eyes may be
> refreshed by a sight of it.*]

Well-lovèd Wiglaf, now the worm is a-lying,   50
Sore-wounded sleepeth, disseized of his treasure.
Go thou in haste that treasures of old I,
Gold-wealth may gaze on, together see lying
The ether-bright jewels, be easier able,
Having the heap of hoard-gems, to yield my
Life and the land-folk whom long I have governed."

XXXVIII. Wiglaf Plunders the Dragon's Den.—Beowulf's Death.

Then heard I that Wihstan's son very quickly,

> [*Wiglaf fulfils his lord's behest.*]

These words being uttered, heeded his liegelord
Wounded and war-sick, went in his armor,
His well-woven ring-mail, 'neath the roof of the barrow.
Then the trusty retainer treasure-gems many
Victorious saw, when the seat he came near to,

> [*The dragon's den.*]

Gold-treasure sparkling spread on the bottom,
Wonder on the wall, and the worm-creature's cavern,
The ancient dawn-flier's, vessels a-standing,
Cups of the ancients of cleansers bereavèd,   10
Robbed of their ornaments: there were helmets in numbers,
Old and rust-eaten, arm-bracelets many,
Artfully woven. Wealth can easily,
Gold on the sea-bottom, turn into vanity[118]
Each one of earthmen, arm him who pleaseth!
And he saw there lying an all-golden banner
High o'er the hoard, of hand-wonders greatest,

---

[118] The word 'oferhígian' (2767) being vague and little understood, two quite distinct translations of this passage have arisen. One takes 'oferhígian' as meaning 'to exceed,' and, inserting 'hord' after 'gehwone,' renders: *The treasure may easily, the gold in the ground, exceed in value every hoard of man, hide it who will.* The other takes 'oferhígian' as meaning 'to render arrogant,' and, giving the sentence a moralizing tone, renders substantially as in the body of this work. (Cf. 28 $_{13}$ et seq.)

Linkèd with lacets: a light from it sparkled,
That the floor of the cavern he was able to look on,
To examine the jewels. Sight of the dragon   20

[*The dragon is not there.*]

Not any was offered, but edge offcarried him.
Then I heard that the hero the hoard-treasure plundered,

[*Wiglaf bears the hoard away.*]

The giant-work ancient reaved in the cavern,
Bare on his bosom the beakers and platters,
As himself would fain have it, and took off the standard,
The brightest of beacons;[119] the bill had erst injured
(Its edge was of iron), the old-ruler's weapon,
Him who long had watched as ward of the jewels,
Who fire-terror carried hot for the treasure,
Rolling in battle, in middlemost darkness,   30
Till murdered he perished. The messenger hastened,
Not loth to return, hurried by jewels:
Curiosity urged him if, excellent-mooded,
Alive he should find the lord of the Weders
Mortally wounded, at the place where he left him.
'Mid the jewels he found then the famous old chieftain,
His liegelord belovèd, at his life's-end gory:
He thereupon 'gan to lave him with water,
Till the point of his word piercèd his breast-hoard.
Beowulf spake (the gold-gems he noticed),   40
The old one in sorrow: "For the jewels I look on

[*Beowulf is rejoiced to see the jewels.*]

Thanks do I utter for all to the Ruler,
Wielder of Worship, with words of devotion,
The Lord everlasting, that He let me such treasures
Gain for my people ere death overtook me.
Since I've bartered the agèd life to me granted
For treasure of jewels, attend ye henceforward
The wants of the war-thanes; I can wait here no longer.

---

[119] The passage beginning here is very much disputed. 'The bill of the old lord' is by some regarded as Beowulf's sword; by others, as that of the ancient possessor of the hoard. 'Ær gescód' (2778), translated in this work as verb and adverb, is by some regarded as a compound participial adj. = *sheathed in brass.*

[He desires to be held in memory by his people.]

The battle-famed bid ye to build them a grave-hill,
Bright when I'm burned, at the brim-current's limit;   50
As a memory-mark to the men I have governed,
Aloft it shall tower on Whale's-Ness uprising,
That earls of the ocean hereafter may call it
Beowulf's barrow, those who barks ever-dashing
From a distance shall drive o'er the darkness of waters."
The bold-mooded troop-lord took from his neck then

[The hero's last gift

The ring that was golden, gave to his liegeman,
The youthful war-hero, his gold-flashing helmet,
His collar and war-mail, bade him well to enjoy them:
"Thou art latest left of the line of our kindred,   60

and last words.]

Of Wægmunding people: Weird hath offcarried
All of my kinsmen to the Creator's glory,
Earls in their vigor: I shall after them fare."
'Twas the aged liegelord's last-spoken word in
His musings of spirit, ere he mounted the fire,
The battle-waves burning: from his bosom departed
His soul to seek the sainted ones' glory.

XXXIX. The Dead Foes.—Wiglaf's Bitter Taunts.

It had wofully chanced then the youthful retainer

[Wiglaf is sorely grieved to see his lord look so un-warlike.]

To behold on earth the most ardent-belovèd
At his life-days' limit, lying there helpless.
The slayer too lay there, of life all bereavèd,
Horrible earth-drake, harassed with sorrow:
The round-twisted monster was permitted no longer

[The dragon has plundered his last hoard.]

To govern the ring-hoards, but edges of war-swords
Mightily seized him, battle-sharp, sturdy
Leavings of hammers, that still from his wounds

The flier-from-farland fell to the earth   10
Hard by his hoard-house, hopped he at midnight
Not e'er through the air, nor exulting in jewels
Suffered them to see him: but he sank then to earthward
Through the hero-chief's handwork. I heard sure it throve then
But few in the land of liegemen of valor,

[*Few warriors dared to face the monster.*]

Though of every achievement bold he had proved him,
To run 'gainst the breath of the venomous scather,
Or the hall of the treasure to trouble with hand-blows,
If he watching had found the ward of the hoard-hall
On the barrow abiding. Beowulf's part of   20
The treasure of jewels was paid for with death;
Each of the twain had attained to the end of
Life so unlasting. Not long was the time till
The tardy-at-battle returned from the thicket,

[*The cowardly thanes come out of the thicket.*]

The timid truce-breakers ten all together,
Who durst not before play with the lances
In the prince of the people's pressing emergency;
But blushing with shame, with shields they betook them,

[*They are ashamed of their desertion.*]

With arms and armor where the old one was lying:
They gazed upon Wiglaf. He was sitting exhausted,   30
Foot-going fighter, not far from the shoulders
Of the lord of the people, would rouse him with water;
No whit did it help him; though he hoped for it keenly,
He was able on earth not at all in the leader
Life to retain, and nowise to alter
The will of the Wielder; the World-Ruler's power[120]
Would govern the actions of each one of heroes,
As yet He is doing. From the young one forthwith then

[*Wiglaf is ready to excoriate them.*]

---

[120] For 'dædum rædan' (2859) B. suggests 'déað árædan,' and renders: *The might (or judgment) of God would determine death for every man, as he still does.*

Could grim-worded greeting be got for him quickly
Whose courage had failed him. Wiglaf discoursed then,   40
Weohstan his son, sad-mooded hero,
Looked on the hated: "He who soothness will utter

[*He begins to taunt them.*]

Can say that the liegelord who gave you the jewels,
The ornament-armor wherein ye are standing,
When on ale-bench often he offered to hall-men
Helmet and burnie, the prince to his liegemen,
As best upon earth he was able to find him,—
That he wildly wasted his war-gear undoubtedly

[*Surely our lord wasted his armor on poltroons.*]

When battle o'ertook him.[121] The troop-king no need had
To glory in comrades; yet God permitted him,   50
Victory-Wielder, with weapon unaided

[*He, however, got along without you.*]

Himself to avenge, when vigor was needed.
I life-protection but little was able
To give him in battle, and I 'gan, notwithstanding,
Helping my kinsman (my strength overtaxing):

[*With some aid, I could have saved our liegelord.*]

He waxed the weaker when with weapon I smote on
My mortal opponent, the fire less strongly
Flamed from his bosom. Too few of protectors
Came round the king at the critical moment.
Now must ornament-taking and weapon-bestowing,   60

[*Gift-giving is over with your people: the ring-lord is dead.*]

Home-joyance all, cease for your kindred,
Food for the people; each of your warriors
Must needs be bereavèd of rights that he holdeth

---

[121] Some critics, H. himself in earlier editions, put the clause, 'When ... him' (A.-S. 'þá ... beget') with the following sentence; that is, they make it dependent upon 'þorfte' (2875) instead of upon 'forwurpe' (2873).

In landed possessions, when faraway nobles
Shall learn of your leaving your lord so basely,
The dastardly deed. Death is more pleasant

[*What is life without honor?*]

To every earlman than infamous life is!"

XL. The Messenger of Death.

Then he charged that the battle be announced at the hedge

[*Wiglaf sends the news of Beowulf's death to liegemen near
by.*]

Up o'er the cliff-edge, where the earl-troopers bided
The whole of the morning, mood-wretched sat them,
Bearers of battle-shields, both things expecting,
The end of his lifetime and the coming again of
The liegelord belovèd. Little reserved he
Of news that was known, who the ness-cliff did travel,
But he truly discoursed to all that could hear him:
"Now the free-giving friend-lord of the folk of the Weders,

[*The messenger speaks.*]

The folk-prince of Geatmen, is fast in his death-bed,   10
By the deeds of the dragon in death-bed abideth;
Along with him lieth his life-taking foeman
Slain with knife-wounds: he was wholly unable
To injure at all the ill-planning monster
With bite of his sword-edge. Wiglaf is sitting,

[*Wiglaf sits by our dead lord.*]

Offspring of Wihstan, up over Beowulf,
Earl o'er another whose end-day hath reached him,
Head-watch holdeth o'er heroes unliving,[122]
For friend and for foeman. The folk now expecteth

[*Our lord's death will lead to attacks from our old foes.*]

---

[122] 'Hige-méðum' (2910) is glossed by H. as dat. plu. (= for the dead). S. proposes
'hige-méðe,' nom. sing. limiting Wigláf; i.e. *W., mood-weary, holds head-watch o'er
friend and foe.*—B. suggests taking the word as dat. inst. plu. of an abstract noun in -'u.'
The translation would be substantially the same as S.'s.

A season of strife when the death of the folk-king   20
To Frankmen and Frisians in far-lands is published.
The war-hatred waxed warm 'gainst the Hugmen,
When Higelac came with an army of vessels

[*Higelac's death recalled.*]

Faring to Friesland, where the Frankmen in battle
Humbled him and bravely with overmight 'complished
That the mail-clad warrior must sink in the battle,
Fell 'mid his folk-troop: no fret-gems presented
The atheling to earlmen; aye was denied us
Merewing's mercy. The men of the Swedelands
For truce or for truth trust I but little;   30
But widely 'twas known that near Ravenswood Ongentheow
Sundered Hæthcyn the Hrethling from life-joys,

[*Hæthcyn's fall referred to.*]

When for pride overweening the War-Scylfings first did
Seek the Geatmen with savage intentions.
Early did Ohthere's age-laden father,
Old and terrible, give blow in requital,
Killing the sea-king, the queen-mother rescued,
The old one his consort deprived of her gold,
Onela's mother and Ohthere's also,
And then followed the feud-nursing foemen till hardly,   40
Reaved of their ruler, they Ravenswood entered.
Then with vast-numbered forces he assaulted the remnant,
Weary with wounds, woe often promised
The livelong night to the sad-hearted war-troop:
Said he at morning would kill them with edges of weapons,
Some on the gallows for glee to the fowls.
Aid came after to the anxious-in-spirit
At dawn of the day, after Higelac's bugle
And trumpet-sound heard they, when the good one proceeded
And faring followed the flower of the troopers.   50

XLI. *The Messenger's Retrospect.*

"The blood-stainèd trace of Swedes and Geatmen,

[*The messenger continues, and refers to the feuds of Swedes and Geats.*]

The death-rush of warmen, widely was noticed,
How the folks with each other feud did awaken.
The worthy one went then[123] with well-beloved comrades,
Old and dejected to go to the fastness,
Ongentheo earl upward then turned him;
Of Higelac's battle he'd heard on inquiry,
The exultant one's prowess, despaired of resistance,
With earls of the ocean to be able to struggle,
'Gainst sea-going sailors to save the hoard-treasure,   10
His wife and his children; he fled after thenceward
Old 'neath the earth-wall. Then was offered pursuance
To the braves of the Swedemen, the banner[124] to Higelac.
They fared then forth o'er the field-of-protection,
When the Hrethling heroes hedgeward had thronged them.
Then with edges of irons was Ongentheow driven,
The gray-haired to tarry, that the troop-ruler had to
Suffer the power solely of Eofor:
Wulf then wildly with weapon assaulted him,

[*Wulf wounds Ongentheow.*]

Wonred his son, that for swinge of the edges   20
The blood from his body burst out in currents,
Forth 'neath his hair. He feared not however,
Gray-headed Scylfing, but speedily quited
The wasting wound-stroke with worse exchange,

[*Ongentheow gives a stout blow in return.*]

---

[123] For 'góda,' which seems a surprising epithet for a Geat to apply to the "terrible" Ongentheow, B. suggests 'gomela.' The passage would then stand: '*The old one went then,*' etc.

[124] For 'segn Higeláce,' K., Th., and B. propose 'segn Higeláces,' meaning: *Higelac's banner followed the Swedes (in pursuit).*—S. suggests 'sæcc Higeláces,' and renders: *Higelac's pursuit.*—The H.-So. reading, as translated in our text, means that the banner of the enemy was captured and brought to Higelac as a trophy.

When the king of the thane-troop thither did turn him:
The wise-mooded son of Wonred was powerless
To give a return-blow to the age-hoary man,
But his head-shielding helmet first hewed he to pieces,
That flecked with gore perforce he did totter,
Fell to the earth; not fey was he yet then,   30
But up did he spring though an edge-wound had reached him.
Then Higelac's vassal, valiant and dauntless,

[*Eofor smites Ongentheow fiercely.*]

When his brother lay dead, made his broad-bladed weapon,
Giant-sword ancient, defence of the giants,
Bound o'er the shield-wall; the folk-prince succumbed then,
Shepherd of people, was pierced to the vitals.

[*Ongentheow is slain.*]

There were many attendants who bound up his kinsman,
Carried him quickly when occasion was granted
That the place of the slain they were suffered to manage.
This pending, one hero plundered the other,   40
His armor of iron from Ongentheow ravished,
His hard-sword hilted and helmet together;
The old one's equipments he carried to Higelac.

[*Eofor takes the old king's war-gear to Higelac.*]

He the jewels received, and rewards 'mid the troopers
Graciously promised, and so did accomplish:
The king of the Weders requited the war-rush,
Hrethel's descendant, when home he repaired him,
To Eofor and Wulf with wide-lavished treasures,

[*Higelac rewards the brothers.*]

To each of them granted a hundred of thousands
In land and rings wrought out of wire: 50
None upon mid-earth needed to twit him[125]

---

[125] The rendering given in this translation represents the king as being generous beyond the possibility of reproach; but some authorities construe 'him' (2996) as plu., and understand the passage to mean that no one reproached the two brothers with having received more reward than they were entitled to.

[*His gifts were beyond cavil.*]

With the gifts he gave them, when glory they conquered;
And to Eofor then gave he his one only daughter,

[*To Eofor he also gives his only daughter in marriage.*]

The honor of home, as an earnest of favor.
That's the feud and hatred—as ween I 'twill happen—
The anger of earthmen, that earls of the Swedemen
Will visit on us, when they hear that our leader
Lifeless is lying, he who longtime protected
His hoard and kingdom 'gainst hating assailers,
Who on the fall of the heroes defended of yore   60
The deed-mighty Scyldings,[126] did for the troopers
What best did avail them, and further moreover
Hero-deeds 'complished. Now is haste most fitting,

[*It is time for us to pay the last marks of respect to our lord.*]

That the lord of liegemen we look upon yonder,
And that one carry on journey to death-pyre
Who ring-presents gave us. Not aught of it all
Shall melt with the brave one—there's a mass of bright jewels,
Gold beyond measure, grewsomely purchased
And ending it all ornament-rings too
Bought with his life; these fire shall devour,   70
Flame shall cover, no earlman shall wear
A jewel-memento, nor beautiful virgin
Have on her neck rings to adorn her,
But wretched in spirit bereavèd of gold-gems
She shall oft with others be exiled and banished,
Since the leader of liegemen hath laughter forsaken,
Mirth and merriment. Hence many a war-spear
Cold from the morning shall be clutched in the fingers,
Heaved in the hand, no harp-music's sound shall
Waken the warriors, but the wan-coated raven   80
Fain over fey ones freely shall gabble,

---

[126] The name 'Scyldingas' here (3006) has caused much discussion, and given rise
to several theories, the most important of which are as follows: (1) After the downfall of
Hrothgar's family, Beowulf was king of the Danes, or Scyldings. (2) For 'Scyldingas'
read 'Scylfingas'—that is, after killing Eadgils, the Scylfing prince, Beowulf conquered
his land, and held it in subjection. (3) M. considers 3006 a thoughtless repetition of 2053.
(Cf. H.-So.)

Shall say to the eagle how he sped in the eating,
When, the wolf his companion, he plundered the slain."
So the high-minded hero was rehearsing these stories
Loathsome to hear; he lied as to few of
Weirds and of words. All the war-troop arose then,

[*The warriors go sadly to look at Beowulf's lifeless body.*]

'Neath the Eagle's Cape sadly betook them,
Weeping and woful, the wonder to look at.
They saw on the sand then soulless a-lying,
His slaughter-bed holding, him who rings had given them   90
In days that were done; then the death-bringing moment
Was come to the good one, that the king very warlike,
Wielder of Weders, with wonder-death perished.
First they beheld there a creature more wondrous,
The worm on the field, in front of them lying,

[*They also see the dragon.*]

The foeman before them: the fire-spewing dragon,
Ghostly and grisly guest in his terrors,
Was scorched in the fire; as he lay there he measured
Fifty of feet; came forth in the night-time[127]
To rejoice in the air, thereafter departing   100
To visit his den; he in death was then fastened,
He would joy in no other earth-hollowed caverns.
There stood round about him beakers and vessels,
Dishes were lying and dear-valued weapons,
With iron-rust eaten, as in earth's mighty bosom
A thousand of winters there they had rested:
That mighty bequest then with magic was guarded,

[*The hoard was under a magic spell.*]

Gold of the ancients, that earlman not any
The ring-hall could touch, save Ruling-God only,
Sooth-king of Vict'ries gave whom He wished to   110
[128](He is earth-folk's protector) to open the treasure,

---

[127] B. takes 'nihtes' and 'hwílum' (3045) as separate adverbial cases, and renders:
Joy in the air had he of yore by night, etc. He thinks that the idea of vanished time ought
to be expressed.
[128] The parenthesis is by some emended so as to read: (1) (*He* (i.e. *God*) *is the hope
of men*); (2) (*he is the hope of heroes*). Gr.'s reading has no parenthesis, but says: ...

[*God alone could give access to it.*]

E'en to such among mortals as seemed to Him proper.

XLII. Wiglaf's Sad Story.—The Hoard Carried Off.

Then 'twas seen that the journey prospered him little
Who wrongly within had the ornaments hidden[129]
Down 'neath the wall. The warden erst slaughtered
Some few of the folk-troop: the feud then thereafter
Was hotly avengèd. 'Tis a wonder where,[130]
When the strength-famous trooper has attained to the end of
Life-days allotted, then no longer the man may
Remain with his kinsmen where mead-cups are flowing.
So to Beowulf happened when the ward of the barrow,
Assaults, he sought for: himself had no knowledge   10
How his leaving this life was likely to happen.
So to doomsday, famous folk-leaders down did
Call it with curses—who 'complished it there—
That that man should be ever of ill-deeds convicted,
Confined in foul-places, fastened in hell-bonds,
Punished with plagues, who this place should e'er ravage.[131]
He cared not for gold: rather the Wielder's
Favor preferred he first to get sight of.[132]
Wiglaf discoursed then, Wihstan his son:

[*Wiglaf addresses his comrades.*]

---

*could touch, unless God himself, true king of victories, gave to whom he would to open
the treasure, the secret place of enchanters, etc.* The last is rejected on many grounds.

[129] For 'gehýdde,' B. suggests 'gehýðde': the passage would stand as above except
the change of 'hidden' (v. 2) to 'plundered.' The reference, however, would be to the
thief, not to the dragon.

[130] The passage 'Wundur ... búan' (3063-3066), M. took to be a question asking
whether it was strange that a man should die when his appointed time had come.—B.
sees a corruption, and makes emendations introducing the idea that a brave man should
not die from sickness or from old age, but should find death in the performance of some
deed of daring.—S. sees an indirect question introduced by 'hwár' and dependent upon
'wundur': *A secret is it when the hero is to die, etc.*—Why may the two clauses not be
parallel, and the whole passage an Old English cry of '*How wonderful is death!*'?—S.'s
is the best yet offered, if 'wundor' means 'mystery.'

[131] For 'strude' in H.-So., S. suggests 'stride.' This would require 'ravage' (v. 16) to
be changed to 'tread.'

[132] 'He cared ... sight of' (17, 18), S. emends so as to read as follows: *He (Beowulf)
had not before seen the favor of the avaricious possessor.*

"Oft many an earlman on one man's account must   20
Sorrow endure, as to us it hath happened.
The liegelord belovèd we could little prevail on,
Kingdom's keeper, counsel to follow,
Not to go to the guardian of the gold-hoard, but let him
Lie where he long was, live in his dwelling
Till the end of the world. Met we a destiny
Hard to endure: the hoard has been looked at,
Been gained very grimly; too grievous the fate that[133]
The prince of the people pricked to come thither.
I was therein and all of it looked at,   30
The building's equipments, since access was given me,
Not kindly at all entrance permitted
Within under earth-wall. Hastily seized I

[*He tells them of Beowulf's last moments.*]

And held in my hands a huge-weighing burden
Of hoard-treasures costly, hither out bare them
To my liegelord belovèd: life was yet in him,
And consciousness also; the old one discoursed then
Much and mournfully, commanded to greet you,
Bade that remembering the deeds of your friend-lord

[*Beowulf's dying request.*]

Ye build on the fire-hill of corpses a lofty   40
Burial-barrow, broad and far-famous,
As 'mid world-dwelling warriors he was widely most honored
While he reveled in riches. Let us rouse us and hasten
Again to see and seek for the treasure,
The wonder 'neath wall. The way I will show you,
That close ye may look at ring-gems sufficient
And gold in abundance. Let the bier with promptness
Fully be fashioned, when forth we shall come,
And lift we our lord, then, where long he shall tarry,
Well-beloved warrior, 'neath the Wielder's protection."   50
Then the son of Wihstan bade orders be given,

[*Wiglaf charges them to build a funeral-pyre.*]

---

[133] B. renders: *That which drew the king thither* (i.e. *the treasure*) *was granted us, but in such a way that it overcomes us.*

Mood-valiant man, to many of heroes,
Holders of homesteads, that they hither from far,
[134]Leaders of liegemen, should look for the good one
With wood for his pyre: "The flame shall now swallow
(The wan fire shall wax[135]) the warriors' leader
Who the rain of the iron often abided,
When, sturdily hurled, the storm of the arrows
Leapt o'er linden-wall, the lance rendered service,
Furnished with feathers followed the arrow."   60
Now the wise-mooded son of Wihstan did summon
The best of the braves from the band of the ruler
Seven together; 'neath the enemy's roof he

[*He takes seven thanes, and enters the den.*]

Went with the seven; one of the heroes
Who fared at the front, a fire-blazing torch-light
Bare in his hand. No lot then decided
Who that hoard should havoc, when hero-earls saw it
Lying in the cavern uncared-for entirely,
Rusting to ruin: they rued then but little
That they hastily hence hauled out the treasure,   70
The dear-valued jewels; the dragon eke pushed they,

[*They push the dragon over the wall.*]

The worm o'er the wall, let the wave-currents take him,
The waters enwind the ward of the treasures.
There wounden gold on a wain was uploaded,

[*The hoard is laid on a wain.*]

A mass unmeasured, the men-leader off then,
The hero hoary, to Whale's-Ness was carried.

---

[134] 'Folc-ágende' (3114) B. takes as dat. sing. with 'gódum,' and refers it to
Beowulf; that is, *Should bring fire-wood to the place where the good folk-ruler lay.*

[135] C. proposes to take 'weaxan' = L. 'vescor,' and translate devour. This gives a
parallel to 'fretan' above. The parenthesis would be discarded and the passage read: *Now
shall the fire consume, the wan-flame devour, the prince of warriors, etc.*

XLIII. The Burning of Beowulf.

The folk of the Geatmen got him then ready

[*Beowulf's pyre.*]

A pile on the earth strong for the burning,
Behung with helmets, hero-knights' targets,
And bright-shining burnies, as he begged they should have them;
Then wailing war-heroes their world-famous chieftain,
Their liegelord beloved, laid in the middle.
Soldiers began then to make on the barrow

[*The funeral-flame.*]

The largest of dead-fires: dark o'er the vapor
The smoke-cloud ascended, the sad-roaring fire,
Mingled with weeping (the wind-roar subsided)   10
Till the building of bone it had broken to pieces,
Hot in the heart. Heavy in spirit
They mood-sad lamented the men-leader's ruin;
And mournful measures the much-grieving widow
*   *   *   *   *   *   *
*   *   *   *   *   *   *
*   *   *   *   *   *   *
*   *   *   *   *   *   *
*   *   *   *   *   *   *
*   *   *   *   *   *   *   20
The men of the Weders made accordingly

[*The Weders carry out their lord's last request.*]

A hill on the height, high and extensive,
Of sea-going sailors to be seen from a distance,
And the brave one's beacon built where the fire was,
In ten-days' space, with a wall surrounded it,
As wisest of world-folk could most worthily plan it.
They placed in the barrow rings and jewels,
All such ornaments as erst in the treasure

[*Rings and gems are laid in the barrow.*]

War-mooded men had won in possession:
The earnings of earlmen to earth they entrusted,   30
The gold to the dust, where yet it remaineth
As useless to mortals as in foregoing eras.
'Round the dead-mound rode then the doughty-in-battle,
Bairns of all twelve of the chiefs of the people,
More would they mourn, lament for their ruler,

[*They mourn for their lord, and sing his praises.*]

Speak in measure, mention him with pleasure,
Weighed his worth, and his warlike achievements
Mightily commended, as 'tis meet one praise his
Liegelord in words and love him in spirit,
When forth from his body he fares to destruction.   40
So lamented mourning the men of the Geats,
Fond-loving vassals, the fall of their lord,
Said he was kindest of kings under heaven,

[*An ideal king.*]

Gentlest of men, most winning of manner,
Friendliest to folk-troops and fondest of honor.

Addenda

Several discrepancies and other oversights have been noticed in the H.-So. glossary. Of these a good part were avoided by Harrison and Sharp, the American editors of Beowulf, in their last edition, 1888. The rest will, I hope, be noticed in their fourth edition. As, however, this book may fall into the hands of some who have no copy of the American edition, it seems best to notice all the principal oversights of the German editors.

From hám (194).—Notes and glossary conflict; the latter not having been altered to suit the conclusions accepted in the former. **Þær gelýfan sceal dryhtnes dóme** (440).—Under 'dóm' H. says 'the might of the Lord'; while under 'gelýfan' he says 'the judgment of the Lord.'

Eal bencþelu (486).—Under 'benc-þelu' H. says *nom. plu.*; while under 'eal' he says nom. sing.

Heatho-ræmas (519).—Under 'ætberan' H. translates 'to the Heathoremes'; while under 'Heatho-ræmas' he says 'Heathoræmas reaches Breca in the swimming-match with Beowulf.' Harrison and Sharp (3d edition, 1888) avoid the discrepancy.

Fáh féond-scaða (554).—Under 'féond-scaða' H. says 'a gleaming sea-monster'; under 'fáh' he says 'hostile.'

Onfeng hraðe inwit-þancum (749).—Under 'onfón' H. says '*he received* the maliciously-disposed one'; under 'inwit-þanc' he says 'he *grasped,*' etc.

Níð-wundor séon (1366).—Under 'níð-wundor' H. calls this word itself *nom. sing.*; under 'séon' he translates it as accus. sing., understanding 'man' as subject of 'séon.' H. and S. (3d edition) make the correction.

Forgeaf hilde-bille (1521).—H., under the second word, calls it instr. dat.; while under 'forgifan' he makes it the dat. of indir. obj. H. and S. (3d edition) make the change.

Brád and brún-ecg (1547).—Under 'brád' H. says 'das breite Hüftmesser mit bronzener Klinge'; under 'brún-ecg' he says 'ihr breites Hüftmesser mit blitzender Klinge.'

Yðelíce (1557).—Under this word H. makes it modify 'ástód.' If this be right, the punctuation of the fifth edition is wrong. See H. and S., appendix.

Sélran gesóhte (1840).—Under 'sél' and 'gesécan' H. calls these two words accus. plu.; but this is clearly an error, as both are nom. plu., pred. nom. H. and S. correct under 'sél.'

Wið sylfne (1978).—Under 'wið' and 'gesittan' H. says 'wið = near, by'; under 'self' he says 'opposite.'

þéow (2225) is omitted from the glossary.

For duguðum (2502).—Under 'duguð' H. translates this phrase, 'in Tüchtigkeit'; under 'for,' by 'vor der edlen Kriegerschaar.'

þær (2574).—Under 'wealdan' H. translates þær by 'wo'; under 'mótan,' by 'da.' H. and S. suggest 'if' in both passages.

Wunde (2726).—Under 'wund' H. says 'dative,' and under 'wælbléate' he says 'accus.' It is without doubt accus., parallel with 'benne.'

Strengum gebæded (3118).—Under 'strengo' H. says 'Strengum' = mit Macht; under 'gebæded' he translates 'von den Sehnen.' H. and S. correct this discrepancy by rejecting the second reading.

Bronda be láfe (3162).—A recent emendation. The fourth edition had 'bronda betost.' In the fifth edition the editor neglects to change the glossary to suit the new emendation. See 'bewyrcan.'

THE END

97292674R00092

Made in the USA
Lexington, KY
28 August 2018